new zealand
skiing and
snowboarding
guide

new zealand
skiing and
snowboarding
guide

Rex Gould

REED

Also by Rex Gould
Top New Zealand Golf Courses

REED PUBLISHING (NZ) LTD
TE KARUHI TĀ TĀPUI O REED (AOTEAROA)

Established in 1907, Reed is New Zealand's largest
book publisher, with over 600 titles in print.
www.reed.co.nz

Published by Reed Books, a division of Reed Publishing (NZ) Ltd, 39 Rawene Road,
Birkenhead, Auckland 10. Associated companies, branches and representatives
throughout the world.

ISBN-13: 978 0 7900 1050 2
ISBN-10: 0 7900 1050 X

First published 2006

National Library of New Zealand Cataloguing-in-Publication Data
Gould, Rex.
New Zealand skiing and snowboarding guide / Rex Gould.
ISBN-13: 978-0-7900-1050-2
ISBN-11: 0-7900-1050-X
1. Ski runs—New Zealand—Guidebooks. 2. Ski resorts—New
Zealand—Guidebooks. 3. Skis and skiing—New Zealand—
Guidebooks. 4. Snowboarding—New Zealand—Guidebooks.
I. Title.
796.930993—dc 22

Designed by Jason Anscomb
Edited by Jeremy Sherlock

Printed in China

NORTH ISLAND 8

NELSON/MARLBOROUGH & CANTERBURY 30

MACKENZIE COUNTRY 74

SOUTHERN LAKES DISTRICT 98

ACKNOWLEDGEMENT

ACKNOWLEDGEMENTS

Putting this book together would not have been possible without the help of many people.

Special thanks must go to the management and staff of the ski areas and heli-ski operators featured in this skiing and snowboarding guide. Thank you all for helping me by supplying information and images, and for those of you who gave time out of your busy schedules to talk to me during visits to your areas.

I wish to acknowledge the contributions and work of the many professional and amateur photographers who have supplied images to each of the ski areas.

To all the staff at Reed Publishing who have helped and guided me through this project, a big thank you. Peter Dowling, thanks for your wisdom and positive can-do attitude, and Jeremy Sherlock, for your marvellous organisational and editorial skills.

I'm not usually into dedications but I would like to pay tribute to all the ski patrol and medical staff, many of whom are volunteers at ski areas around the country.

In particular, thanks to the patrol and medical staff at Turoa and to the National Bank Rescue Helicopter crew for getting me to Palmerston North Hospital in quick time a couple of years ago when I suffered from concussion.

A lesson learned from this escapade was to always wear a helmet, it may save your life. I believe it saved mine.

INTRODUCTION

A LIFELONG LOVE OF THE MOUNTAINS

My first introduction to the mountains came at the age of 12 when my parents, who were avid golfers, took us to Mt Ruapehu during a school holiday break, where we stayed at the Chateau Tongariro. A day or two was spent in the snow near the 'Top o' the Bruce' at Whakapapa and I was hooked.

The following year I pestered Mum and Dad to take us on another trip to Ruapehu. They were not keen but in the end relented to my constant pleas, sending me on my own by train to National Park and then by private taxi to the Chateau. To me it was a dream and one of my fond childhood skiing holiday memories.

During ensuing years I made regular trips to the mountain, staying at ski club lodges with friends, even joining as a foundation member of the Desert Alpine Club at Tukino, a club ski area on Ruapehu's eastern slopes.

My passion for skiing and the mountains has continued, with annual visits to Mt Ruapehu or the South Island ski areas, and the odd pilgrimage to the Okanagan ski areas in British Columbia, Canada.

A few years ago I became a member of Rangatira Alpine Sports Club. This, plus an understanding wife and a son and daughter showing an interest in skiing and boarding, has allowed me to spend more time on the snow than ever before. I intend to continue for many seasons to come.

The *New Zealand Skiing and Snowboarding Guide* follows on from another book of mine, *Top New Zealand Golf Courses*, now in its third edition. This book is intended to be a factual and informative guide to each of New Zealand's commercial and club ski and snowboarding areas; some heli-ski areas have been included as well. In an effort to remain impartial no revenue at all has been generated by sponsorship or advertising.

Welcome to this, the first edition of the *New Zealand Skiing and Snowboarding Guide*. Enjoy.

Rex Gould

NORTH ISLAND

Auckland, New Zealand's largest city, has an abundance of accommodation, nightlife and activities within easy reach of the city centre. Downtown is a very good place to stay — here you will find all types of hotels: budget to luxury, backpacker hostels and apartments. All around the Viaduct Basin is a variety of superb restaurants, bars and nightclubs and the main shopping thoroughfare, Queen Street, is only a short walk away.

From the Viaduct and wharf area, ferries cross to the North Shore on a regular basis. Bookings for cruises and boat trips to the outlying islands of Auckland Harbour may be made at a number of booking offices downtown.

Within an hour of the central city are a number of top-class golf courses, fishing spots, bathing or surf beaches, native bush reserves, regional parks and walking tracks. Boating and sea-kayaking are right at your doorstep and the indoor ski slope Snowplanet is less than half an hour north on the main highway.

Weather plays an important role in any Mt Ruapehu winter holiday. The mountains of the Tongariro National Park are situated on the North Island's exposed Central Plateau; because of this they are subject to a regular battering from the elements. It pays to have other things to do in the event that the ski areas are closed.

Several towns around Mt Ruapehu have a good range of accommodation from backpacker hostels through to luxury hotels. There are plenty of outdoor activities, such as fishing, golf, canoeing, mountain-biking, thermal spas, bush walks and horse treks, to name but a few.

The National Park is renowned for its excellent hiking tracks and climbing terrain. The Tongariro Crossing is one of the most popular trails in the park though it can be treacherous during winter. As always you should dress warmly and carry snacks with something to drink — even on a short walk. If you are unsure of conditions, or planning a long excursion, check in with park staff at the information centres at Whakapapa Village or Ohakune prior to venturing out.

Whakapapa Village at the base of Whakapapa ski area's access road has several motels, a camping ground and a historic luxury hotel, The Chateau Tongariro.

From the village there are a number of walking and hiking tracks leading out into the national park. Maps of the area and current weather conditions are available from the park's office, located a few hundred metres up the road from the Chateau.

National Park is a township situated at the junction of State Highways 4 and 47. Here you will find lodges, motels and a hotel. If you need gear there are several ski and snowboard rental and retail shops offering an excellent variety of up-to-date equipment. Walking tracks, horse treks, mountain-biking and canoeing excursions are all handy to town.

At the base of Turoa ski area's road is the rural town of Ohakune. There is a good variety of accommodation, plenty of ski and board shops, cafés, restaurants, takeaway food, a supermarket, several bars and yes, even a couple of nightclubs. There are several superb walking tracks to be found a little way up the ski area access road and good trout-fishing streams located within a few minutes of town. For golfers, the Waimarino Golf Course is only five minutes away, midway between Ohakune and the nearby township of Raetihi, which also has accommodation. The military base town of Waiouru is 26 km away at the junction of SH 49 and SH 1 and the site of a very good army museum — educational fun for the whole family.

Turangi is about half an hour from Whakapapa Village and the location of one of the world's best trout-fishing rivers, the Tongariro. Accommodation is plentiful here with everything from camping grounds and motels to fishing lodges. A few minutes from Turangi are the Tokaanu Hot Springs, a great place to relax in a pool or spa after a day on the slopes. The Turangi Golf Course is a good test and welcomes visitors. If you want to entertain the kids a fun and interesting outing is to visit the Trout Hatchery, which you'll find a little south of town on SH 1.

The lakeside resort of Taupo is one of the larger towns in the region, 30–40 minutes north of Turangi. It is a popular holiday destination boasting an array of accommodation, restaurants, cafés and shops. During winter Taupo is a favourite spot for families because it's only an hour or so from the Mt Ruapehu ski areas and there are many other activities to get involved in aside from snow sports. The lake and surrounding rivers provide great fishing and boating with several commercial operators running fishing charters and cruises from the local marina. Wairakei International Golf Course is rated as one of New Zealand's best courses. This, along with Taupo Golf Club's 'Centennial' course, will provide a stern test to players of any ability. Jet boating, bungy jumping, thermal spas, or perhaps a visit to the spectacular Huka Falls are just a few other activities on offer in and around Taupo.

Off the regular tourist routes, Taranaki is not your usual holiday destination, but don't let that put you off visiting the area — there is plenty to do and the people of the region are very friendly. Driving to New Plymouth along the Taranaki Coast, it is easy to see why the rugged shoreline is popular with surfies — it is quite spectacular.

New Plymouth has good accommodation of all varieties, restaurants, bars and all manner of shops together with other city amenities. Known for its gas and oil reserves, Taranaki is largely a farming community so there are quite a few farmstays or homestays around the region where you can stay with local families. If you are skiing or boarding at Mt Taranaki, other accommodation can be had in Stratford, which is in close proximity to the mountain access road.

SNOWPLANET

Life's more fun on
SNOWPLANET™

ADDRESS

Snowplanet, 91 Small Road, Silverdale, Auckland
Telephone: **(09) 427 0044** Email: **bookingsystem@snowplanet.co.nz**
Web: **www.snowplanet.co.nz**

THE FACILITY

Length: 202 metres
Width: 40 metres
Vertical: 30 metres
Gradient: 9–30%

Situated just off the main northern highway 20 minutes from downtown Auckland, Snowplanet has established itself as a worthwhile addition to the New Zealand snow sports industry.

Several attempts have been made over the years to provide a ski and snowboarding venue in Auckland by using artificial surfaces; none of these lasted for very long. People, especially those who were regular winter skiers and boarders, were not attracted to mats or toothbrush-bristle slopes. Snowplanet is a whole new story; here you have a surface which *is* the real thing.

During summer, Snowplanet is a great off-season/pre-season training ground. As an introduction to skiing or boarding it's an excellent place to get started. Located indoors, there is no poor weather, a bonus for those of us who know of the central North Island's fickle conditions. I am told that ski school staff at the Mt Ruapehu ski areas believe the standard of first-timers, many of whom live in Auckland, has improved since the introduction of Snowplanet.

The facility is housed in a building cooled to a constant -5°C. Dress warmly: it may be a summer's day of 25°C outside but remember inside Snowplanet it's below zero. Take your ski jacket, gloves, over-trousers and a warm pair of socks.

A snow academy operates year round, providing instruction to skiers and boarders of all ability levels as well as offering freestyle and race coaching.

Off-snow facilities include a modern rental department, a fully stocked shop with all the latest equipment and a very good restaurant/bar looking out to the snow slope.

Two platter lifts haul patrons to the top of Snowplanet's 200-m trail which is kept in top condition by the use of snowmaking and regular grooming. A magic carpet lift transports newcomers on the beginner's area.

Snowboarders and freestyle skiers have a terrain park featuring several rails, ledges and jumps while downhill skiers and boarders are treated to a slope of reasonable gradient up near the top. It has enough length to carve a few turns at moderate speed before entering a slow-speed zone down towards the base area.

I have to admit to being more than a little skeptical prior to my first visit to Snowplanet; this was probably brought on by previous experiences such as carpet burn on the artificial ski slopes of a former era. To my surprise I found skiing here not too bad. It was not enough to hold my attention for too long — an hour or two would be plenty — but really good to practice a few turns and to get a feel back for the snow after two or three months off.

Snowplanet does not pretend to be big mountain skiing and boarding. Accept the facility for what it is and enjoy it.

SEASON: ALL YEAR ROUND

Terrain Rating

Beginner	65%
Intermediate	25%
Advanced	10%

FACILITIES

- 2 platter lifts
- 1 magic carpet
- Restaurant/bar
- Ski and board rental
- Snow School
- Ski shop

Great:
For beginners. Quite good also for intermediate and advanced as pre-season or off-season practice.

Not so great:
If you're expecting a large variation in terrain.

HOW TO GET THERE

From Auckland City: Take State Highway 1 (northern motorway) over the Auckland Harbour Bridge past Albany and turn off at the Silverdale exit. Take a right turn over the motorway through a roundabout, then right into Small Road. Snowplanet is on your left just past a small fun park.

Snowplanet operate a shuttle service to and from Auckland city hotels. Contact guest services for details.

WHAKAPAPA
SKI AREA

ADDRESS

Whakapapa Ski Area, Mt Ruapehu
Telephone: **(07) 892 3738** Email: **info@mtruapehu.com**
Web: **www.mtruapehu.com**

THE SKI AREA

Elevation: 2300 metres
Base elevation: 1625 metres
Vertical descent: 675 metres
Skiable area: 550 hectares

Located on the north-western slopes of Mt Ruapehu within the Tongariro National Park, mid-way between Auckland and Wellington, Whakapapa is one of New Zealand's largest lift-accessed ski areas.

Operated by Ruapehu Alpine Lifts, the area is unique in that over the years many ski and alpine club lodges have been built above the winter snow line. The interests of commercial operators, mountain club members and the New Zealand public club are monitored by the Department of Conservation — so, as one can imagine, progress on upgrading facilities and services can be a protracted process. Huge weekend crowds during a good ski season will often result in queues for everything from lifts to toilets. If you have the option, ski mid-week, it's a whole different story.

Mt Ruapehu, a solitary mountain in the centre of an island with the ocean not very far away, can be dramatically affected by weather patterns. Brilliant sunshine, whiteouts, blizzard, sleet and rain — I've witnessed it all in one day! Never venture onto this mountain without adequate clothing and equipment and never ski or board outside the patrolled area without checking in with ski patrol or park staff.

Base area facilities are adequate with café, ski and board rental, customer services and a medical centre. A free shuttle bus runs regularly to and from the lower car parks to the base area.

Snow School at Whakapapa consists of a number of products including children's programmes for kids over four years of age, a development centre for those getting started, an advanced learning centre for group-learning clinics or multi-day programmes, and a competitive centre. The adaptive centre is very popular and has helped many physically impaired people into skiing and riding. Helpers and specially adapted equipment are provided.

A bonus to skiing at Whakapapa is that your day pass or season holder's pass is accepted at Turoa Ski Area on the south-western side of the mountain.

SKIING AND BOARDING

Whakapapa offers a great variety of terrain from easy to very difficult. Local aficionados say that if you can ski here you can ski almost anywhere. Terrain varies of course according to snow cover, but here skiers can always find a new slope or chute to test their skills. Freeskiers and snowboarders will find many natural pipes and kickers to satisfy their needs along with a terrain park and half pipe.

Happy Valley is a dedicated beginner's area and a great place to get started. It is easily accessed from the base area and offers a chair and two platter lifts, ski school and café.

Intermediate skiing and boarding is to be had all over the area with some of the best runs on the Valley, Knoll Ridge and Far West T-bars and the Waterfall Express and West Ridge Chairs.

For the experts, Black Magic and several advanced runs out on the Far West T-bar are a real buzz, as are several chutes off the Pinnacles; these can be accessed by traversing left from the top of the Valley T-bar. The High Traverse and McKenzie's Mistake are a couple of local favourites to the right of the Waterfall Express chair.

SEASON: JUNE–NOVEMBER

Terrain Rating

Beginner	20%
Intermediate	55%
Advanced	25%

HOW TO GET THERE

From Auckland: A trip of approximately 4 hours. Take State Highway 1 to Hamilton, SH 3 to Te Kuiti, then SH 4 to National Park. Turn on to SH 47 and follow the signs to Whakapapa Village on SH 48. If traffic is heavy or you are travelling on Friday evening, the city of Hamilton can be a bottleneck. An alternate route can be taken by turning off SH 1 at Ngaruawahia, following on SH 39 through Whatawhata Te Kowhai and Pirongia, and on to SH 31 to Otorohanga and SH 3 to Te Kuiti. It's not much difference in distance, but can be an easier drive.

From Taupo: Take SH 1 to Turangi, then a short drive on SH 41 towards Tokaanu and the turnoff to National Park on SH 47. This route generally takes about 2 hours.

From Wellington: A journey of 4 hours 15 minutes. Take SH 1 through Bulls, Taihape and Waiouru. Turn on to SH 49, through Ohakune pass and on to SH 4 to National Park. Turn on to SH 47 and follow the signs to Whakapapa Village on SH 48.

The access road is 6 km from Whakapapa Village, sealed and non scary. Always carry chains.

Great:
For an excellent variety of terrain and superb learner's areas.

Not so great:
When the weather is bad and that can be often.

FACILITIES

- Chair lifts: 4 double, 1 express quad, 1 quad
- 4 T-bars
- 4 platter lifts
- 6 rope tows
- 8 snow groomers
- Half pipe
- Terrain park
- 30 groomed trails
- 6 cafés
- Snow School
- Crèche
- Ski shop
- Ski and snowboard rental
- Tyre chain hire
- Snowmaking

TUROA
SKI AREA

ADDRESS

Turoa Ski Area, Mt Ruapehu, Ohakune
Telephone: **(06) 385 8456** Email: **info.turoa@mtruapehu.com**
Web: **www.mtruapehu.com**

THE SKI AREA

Elevation: 2322 metres
Base elevation: 1600 metres
Vertical descent: 722 metres
Skiable area: 500 hectares

The highest ski area in New Zealand, Turoa is situated on the south-western slopes of Mt Ruapehu in the central North Island. Although the areas are in close proximity to each other on the same mountain, Turoa offers a quite different alpine experience to neighbouring Whakapapa.

Cold southerlies dump snow regularly (and at times in large amounts) on Turoa's slopes which, because of the area's southerly aspect, do not receive the sun until later in the day. The generally wider volcanic ash-covered slopes of Turoa tend to require less snow cover than Whakapapa. These conditions sometimes help the area off to an early start and late finish to the ski season, which in recent years has even gone through to Christmas!

Apart from one below the car park area, there are no ski club lodges on the mountain at Turoa. Many of these are located in a village on the outskirts of Ohakune, a township at the bottom of the ski area access road.

Turoa Ski Area claims Australasia's longest vertical at 722 m and has some great skiing and boarding, from wide beginner and intermediate slopes, long cruising intermediate and advanced runs through to some exciting off-piste areas. Nine lifts access 500 ha of terrain including one run of 4 km in good snow conditions.

Snow School at Turoa has a range of packages and lesson options for snowboarders and skiers. Children are well catered for with group lessons for four-year-olds up. Kids Explorer is a fun-filled group session for kids above six years of age who are out of the beginner stage and wish to progress to the upper mountain. A one-hour private lesson I had was really good value. The instructor was clear and easy to understand, encouraging and demonstrated technique precisely.

Base facilities are good, with a licensed restaurant and café, ski shop and equipment rental and a beginner's area. I have found that it can get crowded on weekends, so it pays to be on the road very early if you want to get into one of the top car parks and avoid ticketing and lower-lift queues. Whakapapa and Turoa all-mountain and season lift passes are accepted at both areas.

Turoa has become the North Island ski area I frequent the most. The main reason for this is not so much for the skiing but because of the Ruapehu weather. In recent years I've become a fair-weather skier and most Ruapehu regulars will attest to the fact that wind, rain, sleet and snow are a common occurrence there. So when the skiing is called off there are plenty of other activities I can involve myself in here, such as golf and fly fishing, all within a few kilometres of the ski club lodge.

SKIING AND BOARDING

Alpine Meadow beginner facilities near the base area are a great place to start the kids — the slope is very gentle, smooth and close to food and shelter. From here progress can be made to the Wintergarden Platter or on to runs down the Parklane Chair.

Intermediate skiing and boarding at Turoa can be heaven itself, especially in good snow conditions, with numerous runs across the whole area. An excellent warm-up for the day is to take the Movenpick Chair and move off to the left across Blyth Flat. After crossing under the Giant Chair, drop left into Bone Yard, following the valley down to the bottom station of the Giant. Once at the top of the High Noon T-bar ski off to the right and on to Vertigo. The upper end of this run is really good skiing; at about half-way veer a little right toward the T-bar and then take a line down which brings you to the left of the bottom station. Off to the left at the top of the High Noon is a cat track which takes you over to intermediate runs either side of the Jumbo T-bar. In between you'll find superb skiing and boarding by dropping into Little Bowl and Big Bowl.

Advanced riders and skiers will find great skiing and boarding off the top of the High Noon and over to the right where Triangle, Muzzazone or Hamilton's Face await you. A little further over the lower Mangaehuehu Glacier, you move into a back-country area where new lines can often be had in fresh or wind-blown powder. Always seek ski patrol clearance before venturing out there.

Freestylers on one or two boards will enjoy the variety of the terrain park at Turoa with a number of hits, bumps, boxes, rails and jumps. The wide open slopes of the area and a number of natural bowls and jumps make for great free skiing and boarding too.

SEASON: JUNE–NOVEMBER

Terrain Rating

Beginner	25%
Intermediate	50%
Advanced	25%

HOW TO GET THERE

From Auckland: Take State Highway 4 through Taumarunui and National Park, then SH 49 to Ohakune. It should take approximately 4 hours 30 minutes.

From Wellington: Follow SH 1 to Taihape and at Waiouru take SH 49 to Ohakune — a journey of around 4 hours.

Turoa Ski Area is 17 km from the centre of Ohakune or around 20–25 minutes driving time. The access road is sealed, well-maintained and provides a chain hire service.

Shuttle services run at regular intervals up and down the mountain. Check with local ski shops: most will help with bookings or put you in touch with a shuttle company.

Great:
For wide open cruising runs. A couple of nice bowls up top. Fairly reliable snow cover.

Not so great:
When the weather is rough, especially during north-westerly or southerly storms.

FACILITIES

- Chairlifts: 2 quad, 2 triple
- 2 T-bars
- 3 platter lifts
- Snowmaking
- Terrain park
- 5 groomers
- 3 cafés
- Snow School
- Equipment rental
- Medical centre
- Shop

TUKINO

ADDRESS

Tukino, Mt Ruapehu, Tongariro National Park Telephone: **0800 885 466**
Email: **information@tukino.co.nz** Mountain Manager: **(06) 387 6294**
Web: **www.tukino.co.nz**

THE SKI AREA

Elevation: 1890 metres
Base elevation: 1650 metres
Vertical descent: 250 metres
Skiable area: 19 hectares

In his book *Ski Resorts of the World*, author Arnie Wilson describes the list of facilities at Tukino as "unsettling reading". He goes on to describe Tukino's approach road as one of the most difficult in the country with Mt Ruapehu and Treble Cone the best of our ski areas. Arnie, who doesn't appear to have skied in New Zealand, obviously prefers skiing on the groomed corduroy pistes of St Moritz, sipping champagne and caviar back in his hotel room, to the ungroomed back-country skiing and club -lodge camaraderie that exists at the many club-operated ski areas such as Tukino. Come to New Zealand Arnie, I'll show you where to find a couple of *really* difficult approach roads!

A 7 km drive from the Desert Road on State Highway 1 on the sheltered eastern side of Mt Ruapehu, Tukino ski area is operated by the Desert Alpine and Aorangi Ski Clubs. On a clear day there are magnificent views north to Mt Ngauruhoe and eastward to the Kaimanawa Ranges.

For me, this is where it all began. Tukino is where I was as first introduced by a friend to skiing and ski club life with the Desert Alpine Club. Many a fond memory I have of mixing concrete, lifting timber, snoring on the floor with 20 others after a few drinks too many, pushing Mum's old Austin A35 up the hill through three feet of snow, digging out the club's old ex-army 4WD and learning to ski on straight 215s with leather boots. Those were great times.

How things have changed. Or have they? Apart from the vast improvements in vehicles and ski/boarding equipment, much of the old charm that Tukino had back in the late '60s and early '70s still appears to be there.

Skiers and snowboarders are welcome for the day, although you should check road conditions with area staff prior to driving up the hill; usually 4WD vehicles only are permitted. Transport from the base camp area can often be arranged in advance.

There are no equipment rental or caféteria facilities at Tukino so be prepared and take your own gear, snacks and refreshments. There are also no crowds and no queues.

The most likely scenario for those making the trip to Tukino is to stay a night or two, or even a week on the mountain. Non-members are welcome with both clubs offering packages that include accommodation and meals. You will need to take a sleeping bag, towel, clothing and the usual personal stuff. The lodges of the Aorangi Ski Club and Desert Alpine Clubs are both very comfortable, providing all the home comforts required during your stay on the mountain. As with most ski clubs, daily duties are rostered, with even the kids doing chores, such as peeling spuds or washing the dishes. Yes Mum, you will not believe it!

The Tukino Snow School offers ski and boarding instruction to any level, each lesson customised to suit the ability of students, the terrain and snow conditions. Tukino also has a development squad that provides ski and snowboard training for children and young adults.

SKIING AND BOARDING

Tow belts are provided with the purchase of a lift ticket for the two nutcracker tows that serve the area with a vertical of 250 m. Most of the publicity I've read rates Tukino as having only 5 percent advanced terrain and 65 percent beginner. This may be true if you stay in the direct vicinity of the tows, but much more advanced skiing and boarding is to be found a little further out.

The Whangaehu Tow is located just above and to the left of the lodges providing beginners with a wide gentle slope of around 700 m in length. This is an ideal training ground and a good tow to become familiarised with the use of a nutcracker. During earlier times this tow continued a couple of hundred metres further on to the slopes above. These slopes can be accessed by foot or by traversing across from the Aorangi Tow, where you will find a nice run through the gut and down The Wall to the bottom of the Whangaehu Tow.

Aorangi Tow has good skiing and boarding close to the tow line before a good steep pitch named Shirt Front just before the bottom of the tow. In good snow conditions the chutes are great advanced skiing and boarding. This line will take you down into a river valley below the lodges; from here a walk out is required.

Tukino has some great off-piste terrain. Ski patrols provide ski and snowboarding tours outside the main area. They will help you to find that hidden pocket of wind-blown powder, chutes, jumps, natural pipes and kickers and where to make first tracks.

Be careful when visiting Tukino because someone may thrust a club membership application form under your nose — you might just be tempted to write out the cheque!

HOW TO GET THERE

From Auckland and Taupo: Take State Highway 1 through Turangi and Rangipo and on to the Desert Road. Just over 46 km from Turangi is a signpost on the right to Tukino.

From Wellington: Follow State Highway 1 through Waiouru along the Desert Road for just over 22 km to a signpost on the left to Tukino.

Follow this access road across country for 7 km to the base camp car park.

Do not attempt to drive above base camp until you have confirmed that the road is open either online or by phoning the office. The 7-km mountain road above base camp is for 4WD vehicles only.

Great:
For its lack of crowds and a friendly ski club atmosphere.

Not so great:
For those who dislike nutcracker tows and for difficult access during heavy snow conditions.

FACILITIES

- 2 rope tows
- Snow School
- Ski patrol
- On-mountain accommodation

SEASON: JULY–OCTOBER

Terrain Rating

Beginner	65%
Intermediate	30%
Advanced	5%

MANGANUI
SKI AREA

❄

ADDRESS

Stratford Mountain Club, Mt Taranaki
Telephone: **(06) 765 5493; (027) 280 0860** Email: **smcsec@hotmail.com**
Web: **www.snow.co.nz/manganui**

THE SKI AREA

Elevation: 1680 metres
Base elevation: 1260 metres
Vertical descent: 420 metres
Skiable area: 60 hectares

From a distance the steep conical shape of Mt Taranaki on the North Island's west coast seems an unlikely place to find a ski area. However, the Stratford Mountain Club has a lodge, T-bar and two rope tows located on the mountain's eastern slopes, where some partly forgiving terrain can be found.

A scenic drive of less than one hour from the city of New Plymouth brings you to a sealed access road that winds its way up through the native forest of Egmont National Park to the car park. From your vehicle it's a 20-minute walk around the Manganui Gorge to the base area. A goods lift is available for transporting equipment across the gorge.

Base facilities are adequate for this small, usually uncrowded ski and boarding area. Here you will find a day lodge that provides all the necessities including ticketing, food and drinks.

Ski School is a small personal operation and like the area's lift fees, is real value for money. If you do not have your own equipment there are no rental facilities — you can hire gear from the Mountain House Lodge located 3 km down the access road. Mountain House Lodge provides hotel and motel accommodation, a restaurant and bar.

The Stratford Mountain Club has a modern 32-bed lodge located right on the slopes. Although accommodation is advertised as members only, I am told that the club does accept bookings from non-members. Remember that this is a ski club and as such visitors are asked to assist with light duties. Meals are self-catered so food will need to be carried in. You will also need a sleeping bag.

SKIING AND BOARDING

Coastal weather patterns around Mt Taranaki play a large part as to when the Manganui Ski Area opens and closes. Snow can be scarce at times so my advice is to always check with the Stratford Mountain Club before venturing on a journey of any length.

Loading stations for both the learner's tow and T-bar are situated close to the lodge area, as is the goods lift terminal, where you can unload any equipment you may have sent up from the car park.

Manganui's base area is located on a tussock-covered plateau. This grassy slope is kept in great shape by the voluntary labour of Stratford Mountain Club members; it requires very little snow cover to become operational and is perfect beginner and intermediate terrain.

With a gentle slope on either side, the slow pace of the learner's rope tow is very easy for children or adults new to the snow to manage. The T-bar has a couple of good intermediate runs down the lift line which will even suit confident beginners. In favourable snow conditions, Niagra Gully presents good snowboarding territory with a number of natural hits and jumps.

A nutcracker tow belt is required to negotiate the steeper Top Tow, from the summit of which are a number of runs mostly suiting very strong intermediate to expert skiers and snowboarders. Always check out snow conditions and visibility with lift staff before riding the tow. If conditions are icy, don't bother.

SEASON: JUNE–OCTOBER

Terrain Rating

Beginner	5%
Intermediate	30%
Advanced	65%

FACILITIES

- 1 T-bar
- 3 rope tows
- 1 groomer
- Caféteria
- Shelter
- Goods lift
- Ski School
- Rental equipment (from Mountain House Lodge, 3 km below car park)
- On-mountain accommodation (Stratford Mountain Club Lodge)

Great:
If there is any snow or for something a little different if you happen to be in the area.

Not so great:
If the weather is foul and/or snow conditions are icy.

HOW TO GET THERE

From New Plymouth: It's a 45-minute (54 km) drive on State Highway 3 through Inglewood and Stratford. Just south of Stratford is the access road turn-off and a scenic drive on sealed road to the car park.

From Auckland: New Plymouth is a 355-km gruelling drive. In my opinion making a special skiing or snowboarding trip to Manganui from Auckland is probably not an option, especially considering that Mt Ruapehu is more easily accessible and has much more reliable snow conditions. However, if you are in the area on holiday or just passing through, on a clear day it's worth a visit.

NELSON/MARLBOROUGH AND CANTERBURY

Visitors to Rainbow Ski Area can choose accommodation options from several locations in the Nelson/Marlborough region.

The inter-island ferry terminals are located in the town of Picton where you will find a very good range of accommodation. Sheltered bays within Queen Charlotte Sound make this a very popular boating area, especially during summer months. At any time of year the Anakiwa and Queen Charlotte walkways offer spectacular trekking and are very accessible from Picton.

Blenheim has become one of New Zealand's premier wine-producing areas and is approximately an hour and a half from Rainbow Ski Area. This vibrant town, located on the main route south, is well known for Marlborough's annual wine festival. Blenheim has very good accommodation, supermarkets, cafés, restaurants and is close to the walking tracks of Mt Richmond Forest Park and others in the Wairau Valley or Queen Charlotte Sound. If you fancy a round of golf the Rarangi Golf Club's course is a short drive from Blenheim, out near Rarangi Beach.

Nelson services a wide community and has a population of just over 50,000. Also roughly an hour and a half from Rainbow Ski Area, the town has plenty of accommodation together with all the usual amenities expected for a town of this size. From Nelson there are a variety of outdoor pursuits such as canoeing, sea-kayaking, trekking, golf, mountain-biking and climbing to be enjoyed. Mt Richmond Forest Park, Abel Tasman National Park, North-west Nelson Forest Park, Kahurangi and Nelson Lakes national parks are all within easy reach of town.

St Arnaud is a small holiday town on the shores of Lake Rotoiti only a half-hour's drive from the ski area. There are a number of accommodation options in or around St Arnaud. It is a great place to base yourself for a couple of nights to experience the very good skiing or snowboarding at Rainbow, or maybe even take on one of the many awesome walks available in the surrounding area.

On the South Island's rugged east coast, the seaside town of Kaikoura is world renowned for its Kaikoura whale-watching boating excursions. Motel and hotel accommodation is available in the town as well as a number of homestays or farmstays in the immediate vicinity. For seafood lovers, one the town's main industries is crayfish fishing. Along the coastal road between Blenheim and Kaikoura are several small caravans or shops that sell freshly cooked crayfish to passing motorists.

Mt Lyford's ski area is about an hour from Kaikoura on State Highway 70. Should you wish to stay a night or two, Mt Lyford Village at the base of the area's access road has chalet or lodge-style accommodation, or you can bed down in Kaikoura.

Hanmer Springs is another accommodation option an hour or so south of Mt Lyford. The therapeutic hot springs and spas for which Hanmer is well known are a great place to relax after a hard day's skiing or snowboarding. Hanmer Forest Park has a number of walks while the spectacular St James Walkway is located in Lewis Pass off SH 7.

New Zealand's third-largest city, Christchurch, is located on the coast within an hour to an hour and a half of the Arthur's Pass and Mt Hutt ski areas. Every type of accommodation from budget to luxury can be found in the city together with the usual city nightlife, if that's what you're after. Jet boating, hot-air ballooning, Cashmere Hills cable-car rides, perhaps a romantic Avon River punting (gondola) cruise, world-class golf courses and much more — Christchurch city has it all.

Formerly a small rural town, Methven serviced a predominantly agricultural community; since the development of Mt Hutt Ski Area it has quickly developed into a major Canterbury tourism centre. Backpacker lodges, hotels and motels of all descriptions, together with bars, cafés and restaurants, are located in town. You will also find numerous homestay or farmstay houses out in the community. These are a great way to mix with the locals, especially if you wish to get a real feel for life in rural New Zealand.

Activities such as hot-air ballooning, salmon and trout fishing, jet boating, horse riding, trekking, white-water rafting, farm tours, scenic flights and golf are all available within the immediate area. Mt Hutt Ski Area's access road is only 10 minutes from the centre of town, while Porter Heights and the club ski and boarding areas of Arthur's Pass are only an hour or so driving from Methven.

Other towns close to the six Arthur's Pass ski and boarding areas include Darfield, Springfield and Arthur's Pass Village itself. These small towns all have accommodation of varying types, usually available at very reasonable rates compared to the larger centres.

RAINBOW SKI AREA

ADDRESS

Rainbow Ski Area, Wairau Valley, St Arnaud
Telephone: **(03) 5211861** Email: **info@skirainbow.co.nz**
Web: **www.skirainbow.co.nz**

THE SKI AREA

Elevation: 1760 metres
Vertical descent: 218 metres

In the very north of New Zealand's Southern Alps and overlooking Nelson Lakes National Park is the Rainbow Ski Area. Following an unsuccessful commercial venture, the ski area is now operated by a local community-owned incorporated society.

On a recent trip to the South Island I turned off the main highway at Blenheim headed through vineyard country and up the Wairau Valley to the ski area. The 1½-hour drive was very easy, picturesque and pleasantly lacked the volume of North Island traffic I've become used to.

The area sits on the sunny north-eastern side of a ridge that is sheltered from prevailing west to north-west winds. Because of this aspect Rainbow often gets some large snow dumps from westerly and north-westerly storms while other areas often miss out. At the time of this visit most South Island ski areas had little in the way of snow cover; to my surprise Rainbow had plenty.

Although the area has very few lifts, don't be frightened off by the apparent lack of uphill capacity. As yet Rainbow is relatively undiscovered and at most times you will not find huge crowds of people, especially mid-week.

Base facilities are quite adequate with a café, rental shop and shelter. Importantly, all the area staff I met were well informed, friendly and very helpful.

Skiing and boarding is a fun affair here with a real family or ski club feel to it. Everyone seems to know someone else and it's easy to strike up a conversation with one of the locals, especially if you show an interest in the area and its history.

SKIING AND BOARDING

No super pipes or terrain parks here, but what you do get is very good skiing and boarding on groomed main trails with some very challenging skiing and boarding off trail. At Rainbow you also get maximum vertical for your money; the price of a lift pass is a little more than half that of the large commercial areas.

Intermediates will find good skiing and riding down Roller-Coaster or Harry's Way before descending into Easy Way Home, or taking on the Shirt Front descent back to the T-bar base area.

I noticed several boarders and twintippers getting some big air off natural bumps and jumps out to the left of the T-bar over in an area known as The Planets.

The East Face, advanced territory out to the right of the T-bar, may be accessed off Harry's Way or Allan's Way. You can also find some very challenging terrain by traversing out left to West Bowl. Once there you could find that the further reaches of this bowl may have to be accessed on foot. This area of the mountain is great powder country and looks to have some really good potential for future lift development.

For those people who are just starting into the skiing or snowboarding learning process, there are two tows near the base area, one near the lodge and another in front of the café. Once some confidence is gained you may wish to choose a quiet time to advance to the T-bar where there are some good beginner trails, and your skiing or boarding career will have truly begun.

FACILITIES

- 1 T-bar
- 1 handle tow
- 1 rope tow
- Café
- Ski and board rental
- Ski and Snowboard School
- Snow groomer
- Snowmaking

If you are planning a South Island boarding or skiing road trip I would have to recommend Rainbow Ski Area as a must-do. It is a truly great way to begin or end your holiday.

HOW TO GET THERE

From Blenheim: Take State Highway 6 to Woodbourne and Renwick, then turn off onto SH 63 for an easy drive through the Wairau Valley. The turn-off to Rainbow is on your left just before St Arnaud. The sealed access road crosses several fords before turning off to the right up into beech forest, then on to the ski area.

From Nelson: Travel through Stoke and Richmond, then on to SH 6 to Kawatiri where you turn left along the Buller River to St Arnaud. A little past St Arnaud, turn right onto the ski area access road as per the directions above.

Rainbow Ski Area's access road is relatively easy compared to some, but be careful during mid-winter; tyre chains may be required especially near or above the snow line.

SEASON: ❄
JULY–OCTOBER

Terrain Rating

Beginner	25%
Intermediate	55%
Advanced	20%

Great:
Beginner and intermediate runs. Good off-trail advanced riding.

Not so great:
A little off the beaten track unless you live locally.

MT LYFORD
ALPINE RESORT

ADDRESS

Mt Lyford Alpine Resort, Waiaiu, North Canterbury
Telephone: (03) 315 6178 Email: lyfordski@xtra.co.nz
Web: www.mtlyford.co.nz

THE SKI AREA

Elevation: 1750 metres
Base elevation: 1510 metres
Vertical descent: 450 metres

Situated at the southern end of the seaward Kaikoura Ranges, an hour and a half north of Christchurch and about 50 minutes from Kaikoura, Mt Lyford Ski Area has a hardcore following of local skiers and boarders. It's also developing a reputation amongst visitors travelling to or from the more renowned Canterbury and Southern Lakes ski areas.

Two rope tows, two platters, a poma and a T-bar move people quickly and efficiently around the mountain, dispersing skiers and boarders over a wide area. Lift lines are minimal at weekends and, blissfully, almost non-existent during the week.

Base facilities are quite adequate with a café and day lodge serving good food and drinks, ticketing, a first aid area and the ski and board rental department. I found the staff in all departments to be knowledgeable, helpful and very friendly.

Mt Lyford's terrain park features are constantly upgraded and the use of a mechanical shredder ensures top shaping of the half and quarter pipes.

Snow School at Mt Lyford offers a range of learning options featuring one-or two-hour group sessions, private lessons and full packages which include lesson, lift pass and rental equipment.

The upper slopes of Mt Terako, the area's highest point at 1750 m, have hosted several powder eight competitions; even during lean snow years they hold snow very well. Lyford's lower slopes are well groomed and a great training ground for beginner or intermediate skiers and boarders.

For anyone travelling to or from the North Island on a winter holiday I can highly recommend Mt Lyford as a ski and snowboarding stopover. A great place to stay is The Mt Lyford Lodge, located at the bottom of the access road.

SKIING AND BOARDING

The Wild Ride Terrain Park at Mt Lyford has a lot of natural and manmade features, giving snowboarders and freestyle skiers an exciting place to hang out. Some of the features in the park are a tabletop, kicker, rails, a fun box and C-rail, plus a couple of 5.5 m log rails. The old International Truck Jump is a great favourite for photo shoots and getting some air.

A platter lift and a fixed-grip tow operate on Mt Lyford's beginner's area, which is situated close to the day lodge and parking area, and has proven to be a very good place for the uninitiated to get started.

For intermediate skiers and boarders the Paradise Valley platter has a couple of good warm-up runs: Georgianna's Delight and Slide to get the day underway, before moving on to more challenging stuff on the Cloudy T-bar. Cruise, a run down the right side of the T-bar, would be an excellent slope to perfect your carving technique.

Getting to the upper slopes of Mt Terako by riding the T-bar and Terako rope tow will bring advanced riders and sliders to Excellerator and Exhibition, two very good adrenalin-pumping runs in powder conditions. Should you need something a little longer, further out wide you could take a line down Die Hard past the top of the learner's tow to meet Easy Street, then on to the base of the Deer Valley Poma.

Stronger intermediate skiers and boarders can play around either side of the Terako Tow, where Thriller will either bring you to the summit of Cloudy T-bar or drop in left to Home Run above the Boardercross course and half pipe. For the fitness freaks there's a good run or two down the Mt Lyford Face, which you can climb from the top of the learner's tow.

I am told that there is some good back-country skiing and boarding to be had at Mt Lyford, outside the ski area boundary. Always check in with ski patrol before venturing out of the patrolled area, take the correct equipment, and never ski out of bounds alone.

HOW TO GET THERE

From Christchurch: Take State Highway 1 to Waipara, then turn left onto SH 7 to Culverden. A short distance past Culverden turn right onto SH 70 and carry on through Waiau for approximately 20 km, to Mt Lyford Village on the left.

From Picton and Kaikoura: SH 1 from Picton and Blenheim will bring you to Kaikoura. Six through Kaikoura, turn off right onto SH 70, drive on for another 50 km of scenic road to Mt Lyford Village on your right.

The Mt Lyford access road winds up through forest before a short exposed steep section above the bushline and just before Stellar Bowl. If you are not used to driving on steep mountain access roads this piece can be a little disconcerting; just keep your eyes on the road ahead and you'll soon be at the top. From Stellar Bowl the road carries on around and up to the car parking and day lodge area. Always carry tyre chains.

Shuttle services operate to and from the slopes from outside Mt Lyford Lodge; contact the ski area for timetables and prices.

Great:
For those travelling to or from Picton, little or no crowds, superb learner's area.

Not so great:
For those who dislike rope tows or T-bars.

FACILITIES

- 1 T-bar
- 1 poma
- 2 platter lifts
- 1 fixed-grip tow
- 1 advanced rope tow
- Terrain park
- Half pipe
- Quarter pipe
- International Truck Jump
- 6 Kassbohrer snow groomers
- 1 half pipe shredder
- Café
- Day lodge
- First aid
- Snow School
- Ski and snowboard rental
- Accommodation lodge

SEASON: JUNE–OCTOBER

Terrain Rating

Beginner	30%
Intermediate	40%
Advanced	30%

TEMPLE
BASIN

ADDRESS

Temple Basin, State Highway 73, Arthur's Pass Canterbury
Telephone: (03) 377 7788
Email: info@templebasin.co.nz Web: www.templebasin.co.nz

THE SKI AREA

Elevation: 1753 metres
Base elevation: 1326 metres
Vertical descent: 427 metres
Skiable area: 320 hectares

Regarded by many as one of the country's premier ski and boarding areas, Temple Basin is situated in the midst of New Zealand's Southern Alps in Arthur's Pass National Park. Whether you are in search of serious big-mountain skiing and boarding in a back-country environment or gentle beginner's terrain to begin a career on the snow, at Temple you will find both and everything in between.

Operated by the Temple Basin Ski Club, you do not have to be a member to use their lifts and facilities, though you may wish to join once you discover the reduced rates members receive and feel the sense of comradeship that exists here.

Ski or snowboard for the day or take advantage of a ski/snowboard week package that includes all accommodation, food, lift fees and instruction. Guests staying at the club lodges are expected to help with rostered light duties, such as housekeeping and meals preparation. It's all great fun on and off the snow with many late nights enjoyed by all; a real social environment unfortunately missing at many of today's busy resort-style ski locations.

For such an isolated location, Temple Basin has very good facilities including two lodges on the snow offering bunk-room accommodation for 120 people. Other amenities include ski and board rental, a café and bar.

Internationally qualified instructors provide a range of instruction from daily group or individual sessions through to full-on weekly programmes. Private lesson prices are extremely reasonable. For more advanced skiers and boarders new to the area, what better way is there to explore the wide variety of runs at Temple Basin than with your own coach and personal guide for an hour or two?

SKIING AND BOARDING

Beginners have a very good variety of terrain available on either side of the Cassidy Tow, or for the more intrepid starter you can access more challenging slopes by riding sections of Temple Tow close to the lodge area. From the top of Temple Tow intermediate or advanced skiers and snowboarders traverse over a ridge before dropping into ride a tow serving the expansive sunny slopes of Downhill Basin, where at most times you will find some of the finest skiing and boarding imaginable.

Southerly and north-westerly storms dump fresh powder at Temple on a frequent basis. Consequently, the several natural basins that make up this area can have untracked slopes for days following a storm. International ski and snowboarding magazine scribes have described the riding at Temple Basin as amongst the best in the world — one even wrote that if he had to snowboard in one area for the rest of his life Temple Basin would be it.

From the top of Downhill Basin you can traverse left across and over a ridge into the upper reaches of an area known as Bill's Basin. The selection of lines descending Bill's are many, including a number of chutes, runs and natural pipes leading down to the base of Temple or Cassidy tows. If you are unfamiliar with the area my advice is to tag along with the locals, who are usually only too willing to show you around.

Temple Basin has the added attraction of night skiing, a hugely popular activity with people staying overnight or for those holidaying on a ski week programme.

The New Zealand Snow Safety Institute run winter courses covering all aspects of snow safety including avalanche awareness, back-country skiing and boarding,

mountaincraft or medical and explosives courses, all leading to ski patrol certification.

There's a heap of back-country skiing and snowboarding to be had in the surrounding mountains, though this is not for the inexperienced or the ill-prepared. Never travel into wilderness areas alone or without an avalanche transceiver and safety gear. Always check out conditions beforehand with the ski patrol.

Great:
For all ability levels, those wanting some of the best skiing and boarding in the country and no crowds.

Not so great:
For those who dislike nutcracker tows or a long walk to the lifts and accommodation.

HOW TO GET THERE

From Christchurch: Take State Highway 73 through Porters Pass and Arthur's Pass. Four kilometres west of Arthur's Pass Village you will find the Temple Basin ski area car park. There is a goods lift located a few hundred metres further along the highway, so before parking your vehicle place your gear on this first — it will help to ease the 45–60-minute walk you have to the base area and ski club lodges.

Be aware that this car park is beside a main highway and theft from unattended vehicles does happen from time to time. To lessen the chances of being broken into, do not leave anything of value in your vehicle.

FACILITIES

- 3 rope tows
- Ski and board rental
- Ski and Snowboard School
- Café
- Bar
- Night skiing and boarding
- On-mountain accommodation

SEASON: LATE JUNE–OCTOBER ❄

Terrain Rating

Beginner	25%
Intermediate	50%
Advanced	25%

CRAIGIEBURN VALLEY SKI AREA

ADDRESS

Craigieburn Valley Ski Area, State Highway 73, Canterbury
Telephone: (03) 365 2514 bookings/info; (03) 318 8711 ski area during season
Email: ski@craigieburn.co.nz Web: www.craigieburn.co.nz

THE SKI AREA

Elevation: 1811 metres
Base elevation: 1308 metres
Vertical descent: 500 metres
Skiable area: 400 hectares

Craigieburn has for many years been widely regarded as one of the best lift-accessed areas in the world for advanced to extreme skiing and boarding. Some of the planet's best skiers and boarders have ridden the powder slopes here and travelled back to New Zealand for more. 'Steep and deep' is a description often given to Craigieburn and as the area's statistics tell, there is 0 percent beginner terrain.

After an easy 10-minute drive up the access road from State Highway 73 and parking your vehicle, a short walk is required to the lodge accommodation area. A little further on is the ticket office where you can pick up a tow belt and then another brief walk to the base of the Bottom Tow.

Skiers and snowboarders can and do visit Craigieburn for the day; my advice is if you have the opportunity, take advantage of a ski week package. The deal for a week includes accommodation in one of the ski club's two lodges, meals, tows, and instruction.

Make sure you take what you need for your day or stay at Craigieburn — there are no ski or snowboard rental facilities. If you are staying overnight pack a sleeping bag, towel, spare clothing and all the other items you may require.

Remember that Craigieburn is a ski club-operated area expect to be rostered on to duties such as cleaning and meal preparation. Pitch in, get involved and be assured of the time of your life. This is skiing as it used to be: go hard all day and fun times late into the night. The camaraderie of skiers and boarders of all age groups here is unreal.

Three high-capacity nutcracker rope tows move skiers and boarders quickly to the upper slopes where the Day Lodge can be found on a ridge above and to the right of Middle Tow. Be sure to pack a camera — the views from up there are brilliant.

SKIING AND BOARDING

Make no mistake, Craigieburn is not for the timid or the faint-hearted; if you are a beginner, you'd be better off elsewhere. However, if you are a confident intermediate or advanced skier, a good snowboarder, an expert, or maybe just a complete nutter who loves jumping off cliffs or skiing near vertical powder runs, then this is the place for you!

Bottom Tow has a bend to the right at about a third of the way up; keep your balance here as this piece can get a little tricky when negotiating it for the first time. Carry on up to the top of Middle Tow. You could get off here and make a couple of warm-up runs down the tow line or, as is more likely, you may wish to carry on up to the summit of the Top Tow and Siberia Basin.

Siberia Basin has some great intermediate skiing and boarding either close to the tow line or out a little wider towards Aeroplane Gulley. Descending to the bottom of the Top Tow, intermediates will find a good comfortable run down the valley to the base station of Middle Tow. Riding back up you will notice a series of small chutes running from right to left across the slope above Middle Tow. These are known as the 1st through to 6th Gut. As fate would have it they get progressively more difficult according to number, and they are a great training ground if you want to really improve your skiing and boarding. Once you have mastered the 6th Gut you'll be ready for anything.

For advanced skiers and riders the mountain is yours. From the Top Tow there is a long traverse over to Hamilton Face where you will often find fresh lines in deep powder right to the loading station of the bottom tow. Above and to the right of the Day Lodge are a set of chutes from which you can carry on down to the bottom of Middle Basin. From there it is a 20-minute walk back to the bottom tow.

The immediate area around Craigieburn contains a huge amount of superb back-country terrain. The hardy types may wish to traverse over to Broken River Ski Area where your Craigieburn lift pass will be accepted. Remember to always consult with ski patrol before leaving the area and to always carry the appropriate equipment, such as an avalanche transceiver, with you.

If you want the closest thing to heli-skiing without the helicopter, try Craigieburn Valley Ski Area — you will not be disappointed.

Great:
Almost exclusively for strong intermediates, experts and adrenalin junkies.

Not so great:
Little room for beginners and nutcracker rope-tow haters.

HOW TO GET THERE

From Christchurch: Take State Highway 73 through Porters Pass and Castle Hill village. Once past the entrance to Broken River Ski Area, carry on for a short distance to Craigieburn's access road on your left. From the highway it is only a 6 km drive but do take it easy. It is a good idea to carry chains, especially if you don't have a 4WD.

The distance from Christchurch is 110 km with a total driving time of around 1½ hours.

FACILITIES

- 3 high-capacity rope tows
- Snow School
- Café
- Bar
- On-mountain accommodation

NELSON/MARLBOROUGH & CANTERBURY

SEASON: JUNE–OCTOBER ❄

Terrain Rating

Beginner	0%
Intermediate	55%
Advanced	45%

BROKEN RIVER

----- Broken River Boundary   ----- Craigieburn Valley Boundary

NEW ZEALANDS LARGEST 'OFF PISTE' SKI AREA

Broken River
SKI-SNOWBOARD-HIRE
www.brokenriver.co.nz

----- Rope Tows	◆ Easiest
----- Walking Required	◆ More difficult
----- Out of controlled area	◆ Mostly difficult

◆ Expert
◆◆ Tricky
◆◆◆ Suicidal

Craigieburn
valley ski area
www.craigieburn.co.nz

ADDRESS

Broken River, Alpine Highway, State Highway 73, Porters Pass
Telephone: (03) 318 8713 Email: ski@brokenriver.co.nz
Web: www.brokenriver.co.nz

THE SKI AREA

Elevation: 1820 metres
Vertical descent: 420 metres
Skiable area: 200 hectares

The name Broken River always comes up during discussions with other skiers about the club areas of New Zealand and for good reason: here you will find it all in big-mountain terrain ranging from the comfortable to the extreme. Broken River and the adjoining area of Craigieburn, with their wide basins and narrow chutes of varying steepness, have been described as heli-skiing terrain without helicopters. Deep powder is often the norm.

Broken River is an easy drive from Christchurch, Methven and other surrounding Canterbury ski areas. Skiers and snowboarders of all ages are welcome for the day, a night or two. Better still, take advantage of a Broken River ski week package.

Broken River is administered by the Broken River Ski Club. The area has three accommodation lodges which vary in style from self-catering backpackers to fully serviced facilities. It should be remembered that these are ski club lodges and not luxury hotels; you will need to bring a sleeping bag, pillow case and other necessary personal stuff (maybe a drink or two!). If you enjoy fun evenings and meeting people then Broken River is for you.

Five electrically driven nutcracker rope tows transport skiers and boarders to the slopes. At first glance using the nutcracker may seem a frightening prospect, but I have found that the area staff, locals or anyone with experience will help with advice if you ask. Once you've mastered it the slopes are yours.

Two beginner tows are situated near the Palmer Day Lodge which provides shelter, snacks and drinks. When conditions permit Broken River provides night skiing and riding under floodlights on the slopes above Palmer Lodge.

The ski school at Broken River provides group lessons for skiers and snowboarders — if you want a really good deal their private lessons are unbelievably inexpensive.

There is no ski and snowboard rental equipment at Broken River so you must organise this before you arrive at the area. It is advisable to carry vehicle tyre chains too, especially if you are staying for a few days during mid winter.

SKIING AND BOARDING

Broken River is heaven for intermediate to expert skiers and boarders. While there are beginner slopes around the day lodge these are limited by comparison to the more advanced runs above.

Slopes out to the left of Rugby Tow are easy and lead down to the day lodge or carry on across to Main Tow, regarded as one of the fastest rope tows in the land. Looking out to the left riding up is Sunny Face: as the name would suggest it gets the sun early in the day and offers good morning snow. To the right is Main Basin and Happy Valley — great skiing and a popular bowl for boarders and freeskiers with lots of natural hits, bumps and jumps.

From the top of Main Tow you can traverse off to the right across to the Ridge Tow and the aptly named Nervous Nob, from where several chutes lead to Happy Valley and the Main Basin. From Nervous Nob the advanced open slopes of Alan's Basin may also be accessed. There you will find excellent skiing and boarding, especially in fresh snow conditions. Alan's Basin in good snow cover also has a great run to the bottom, finishing near the car park and access track. From there it's a walk back to the lodges and access tow area.

For back-country lovers Broken River has some great big mountain terrain outside the boundary. Nearby Craigieburn Ski Area can be accessed along the ridge from Nervous Nob, where your Broken River lift ticket may be used. Before venturing out of the area I strongly advise that you check out conditions with ski patrol.

For great skiing and boarding, fun or relaxing evenings on the mountain, superb staff and club members' hospitality, I can highly recommend Broken River.

FACILITIES

- 5 rope tows
- Ski and board school
- Beginner and intermediate runs groomed
- Day lodge
- Canteen snack food
- On-mountain accommodation

HOW TO GET THERE

From Christchurch: Drive about an hour and a half from Christchurch on State Highway 73 through Sheffield and Springfield, and then 7–8 km past Castle Hill is the turn-off to Broken River on your left.

A 15–20 minute drive through beech forest off SH 73 brings you to the Broken River car park. After loading your gear on to the goods lift, a walk of less than half an hour will bring you to the top unloading station and the accommodation lodges.

There is some transport available to Broken River at certain times. Contact the ski area for schedules and operators.

Great:
For intermediates and experts, powder-hounds, and ski club types.

Not so great:
For those who hate walking, demand only groomed runs, want chairlifts and luxury hotels.

SEASON: JUNE–OCTOBER

Terrain Rating

Beginner	20%
Intermediate	50%
Advanced	30%

MT CHEESEMAN

ADDRESS

Mt Cheeseman, Alpine Highway, State Highway 73, Porters Pass
Telephone: **(03) 344 3247; (03) 318 8794** Snowline Lodge, winter only
Email: **info@mtcheeseman.com** Web: **www.mtcheeseman.com**

THE SKI AREA

Elevation: 1845 metres
Base elevation: 1570 metres
Vertical descent: 293 metres

Operated by the Mt Cheeseman Ski Club, this is one of the closest ski areas to the city of Christchurch, and is also one of the most accessible of the club-operated ski areas.

The scenic mountain road brings you to the car park, which is within easy walking distance to the lifts. Facilities here are very adequate, with two T-bars and a learner tow, a day lodge where food and drinks may be purchased, and an equipment rental department. Children under 10 years of age ski for free on the beginner tow.

Learning to ski or snowboard? A very well-run ski school provides group lessons and individual instruction at very reasonable prices.

For those wishing to stay on the mountain, Forest Lodge is situated on the access road and offers backpacker-style accommodation for 36 guests with the added attraction of a nearby ice-skating rink. Snowline Lodge is located near the lift base area and sleeps 68 people. Meals are provided and guests, in true club spirit, assist with some duties such as meal preparation. Take your own sleeping bag, spare clothing and other necessities. You will need to take your own food if staying in the Forest Lodge Backpackers.

A really good deal is one of Mt Cheeseman's ski week packages. This value-for-money ski holiday includes on-snow accommodation and meals, lifts and instruction.

Mt Cheeseman is a popular area for families and individuals visiting for the day, or for visitors and club members staying overnight or longer in one of the club's two lodges on the mountain. The atmosphere here is very friendly with great camaraderie displayed amongst the people on the mountain and in the lodges during the sometimes lengthy fun-filled evenings.

SKIING AND BOARDING

The wide slopes of Mt Cheeseman's main bowl are situated within a sheltered south- easterly-facing basin, providing beginners and intermediates with a variety of terrain and snow conditions. Powder snow after a storm holds well here, giving more advanced riders great off-piste conditions either within the main basin or outside the area boundary.

The beginner's tow is located at the base area parallel to the main T-bar. The slopes are groomed and gentle, a great place on which to get started. In good snow conditions the more adventurous beginner may wish to try the slopes of the main T-bar.

Intermediate boarders and skiers can improve their technique on the groomed runs of the main T-bar or extend themselves a little by moving to more challenging slopes out a little wider before moving to the Ridge T-bar.

Although much of Mt Cheeseman's terrain is rated intermediate, there are some very good runs from the top of the Ridge T-bar down to the base area, which I think many advanced skiers and riders will enjoy too.

The wide slopes of A Basin, especially those below Mt Cockayne, are a certainty for fresh lines if you are out early after a fresh dump of snow. This run can be accessed by traversing across from the panoramic summit of the Ridge T-bar before dropping into its upper reaches, then descending to the base area.

The ridge to your left riding up on the T-bars has several superb lines and some great natural lips and kickers which will keep the free-skiers and freestyle skiers and boarders going back for more. Grooming staff take great pride in their preparation of a natural terrain park complete with a pipe, hits and jumps.

Mt Cheeseman ski area has some awesome back-country terrain which is easily accessible from the summit of the Ridge T-bar; a walk or climb may be required to get back out though. When venturing out of bounds you should always carry the correct equipment and check with ski patrol on snow conditions first. Ski club members are always helpful with advice on where the best snow is to be had.

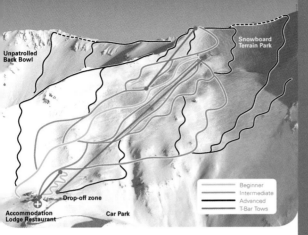

Unpatrolled
Back Bowl

Snowboard
Terrain Park

Drop-off zone

Accommodation
Lodge Restaurant

Car Park

Beginner
Intermediate
Advanced
T-Bar Tows

FACILITIES

- 2 T-bars
- Learner's fixed grip tow
- Quarter pipe and hits
- Groomers
- Day lodge
- Café
- Ski and Snowboard School
- Ski tuning and repairs
- Ski and snowboard rental
- Children's safe area
- Ice skating
- On-mountain accommodation

HOW TO GET THERE

From Christchurch: Take State Highway 73 through Springfield and Porters Pass. The Mt Cheeseman access road is well sign-posted on the left a few kilometres past the Porter Heights Ski Area entrance.

The well-maintained gravel mountain road is an easy drive of 12 km through native beech forest up to the car park. Should you have a lot of gear, I advise you drop this off at an unloading bay up near the base area before going back to the parking area, which is located a couple of hundred metres back down the road.

The road is kept clear of snow but it is advisable to always carry chains.

Great:
For the variety of intermediate terrain and for families.

Not so great:
Advanced skiers and riders may soon crave a bit more variety.

SEASON: JULY–OCTOBER

Terrain Rating

Beginner	15%
Intermediate	50%
Advanced	35%

MT OLYMPUS

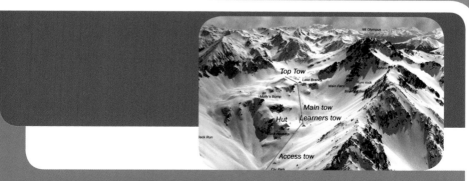

Mt Olympus

Top Tow

Lake Brand

Schism

Rum rock

Main Face

Boulder Belt

-Molly's Bump

Main tow

Learners tow

Hut

Black Run

Access tow

Car Park

ADDRESS

Mt Olympus, Craigieburn Range, Canterbury
Telephone: (03) 318 5840 Email: mtolympus@xtra.co.nz
Web: www.mtolympus.co.nz

THE SKI AREA

Elevation: 1880 metres
Base elevation: 1430 metres
Vertical descent: 450 metres
Skiable area: 60 hectares

Well off the beaten track in a fairly remote area of the Craigieburn Range, Mt Olympus is one of the best kept secrets of New Zealand skiing and boarding. 'Playground of the Gods' is the club's web-site slogan and well it might be, according to many who have been there.

You will not find too many people skiing and boarding at Mt Olympus, in part due to its remote road access and also because the Mt Hutt Ski Area a little further along the main highway has more in the way of lift facilities and is much easier to get to for the masses. Mt Olympus, then, is good for those of us who have an aversion to lift queues and a love of untracked powder snow.

From the car park an access tow transports skiers and boarders up to the Top Hut, which is situated in the middle of the ski area. People do travel up to Mt Olympus for the day, though the best option is to stay for the weekend or join in one of the ski club's weekly packages, which includes on-snow accommodation, meals, instruction and lift fees.

The self-catering backpacker-style Bottom Hut sleeps 12 people, and is very basic, whereas the Top Hut has central heating, a drying room, kitchen and more modern facilities. A chef organises (and sometimes cooks) dinner while all the light duties are carried out by guests and club members. The nightly revelry at Olympus is legendary and if it snows you may be *forced* to stay an extra night or two.

Skiing and snowboarding instruction is available. The private lesson prices at Mt Olympus are incredibly inexpensive. What better way to explore the mountain with only a few other skiers and snowboarders than to do it with your own personal instructor while he or she improves your powder-riding technique?

Facilities include four high-capacity nutcracker rope tows. The Top Hut also acts as the day lodge where you can purchase snacks and drinks from the club cafeteria.

SKIING AND BOARDING

The ski area at Mt Olympus sits in a south-facing bowl on the south-western side of the Craigieburn Range, almost directly opposite several of the other Canterbury club ski areas on the other side of the Craigieburns. This south-facing aspect ensures that Olympus gets a lot of cold dry powder in large dumps and holds it for long periods of time.

A learner's tow can be found outside the lodge alongside the Main Tow; this is a great place to get familiar in the use of a nutcracker. Not as frightening as its name would suggest, the nutcracker is designed to make for an easy ride on high-speed rope tows, once you have mastered the knack of using one.

From the summit of the Main Tow intermediate skiers and snowboarders will find some great runs either side of the tow line. Traverse further out on to the Main Face and you may find a good powder run to the base of Main or further down to the base of the access tow.

In good powder conditions advanced skiers and boarders should try the Back Run. As you reach the summit of Top Tow move off to the left and drop into a long undulating valley of the back basin. Choose your line cruising down and then get on to a great slope carving your way to the base of the access tow.

Mt Olympus has some of the best back-country terrain you will find anywhere in the world. From here you can go cross-country to other ski areas or seek out untracked lines on surrounding mountain peaks; however, it is not for the inexperienced. Always go prepared with the appropriate equipment — in particular, an avalanche transceiver. Never go back-country alone and always check it out with ski patrol first.

Whether you are a beginner, an expert or an extreme skier/boarder, Mt Olympus has plenty of terrain to satisfy the needs of all.

FACILITIES

- 4 rope tows
- Ski and Snowboard School
- Canteen
- Night skiing and boarding
- On-mountain accommodation

HOW TO GET THERE

From Christchurch: Mt Olympus is a 130 km drive. Take State Highway 77 to Windwhistle and turn right, following the signs for around 40 km to the ski area. Upon arriving at the Bottom Hut on the mountain road you will need to radio up to the Top Hut to check the condition of the road; usually 4WD vehicles only should carry on from here. If you are a little jittery driving on steep narrow mountain tracks, it may be better for your nerves to arrange a lift from the Bottom Hut — otherwise it's a 45-minute walk.

During mid winter it is advisable to always check road conditions before heading into the mountains. Always carry chains and a shovel — if it's snowing at Mt Olympus it could be your only way out.

Great:
For lovers of the great wide open, people who make their own fun, powder hounds — no queues, no people.

Not so great:
If you don't like nutcracker rope tows or backpacking your gear to the lodge. If there is a snow storm, there's three feet of powder and you have to get back to your job!

SEASON: JUNE–OCTOBER

Terrain Rating

Beginner	10%
Intermediate	55%
Advanced	35%

PORTER HEIGHTS

ADDRESS

Porter Heights, State Highway 73, Porters Pass
Telephone: (03) 318 4002 Email: ski@porterheights.co.nz
Web: www.porterheights.co.nz

THE SKI AREA

Elevation: 1980 metres
Vertical descent: **620 metres**
Skiable area: 500 hectares

Only an hour's drive from Christchurch, Porter Heights offers great skiing and boarding and is renowned for great powder days. It also has one of the longest vertical runs in the southern hemisphere. Whether you enjoy groomed wide open cruising, cutting new lines down 38-degree snow faces or revelling in back-country powder, most often you'll find it at Porter Heights.

With three high-speed T-bars transporting skiers and boarders up the mountain quickly and efficiently, overcrowding is a rare occurrence. Breathtaking views out over Lake Coleridge to Mt Cook on a clear day are only a short walk above the No. 3 T-bar.

Porter Heights offers great concessions. For example, kids less than 10 years of age and accompanied by an adult ski or board for free. The licensed café has good food, views from the deck and a great atmosphere. The area allows families and groups to bring their own barbecue for car-park lunches — just one small detail that adds to the friendliness of the place.

The comprehensive ski and snowboarding school has a range of instruction, including two-hour group beginners' sessions, one-hour private lessons and even a half-hour carving tips session. There is also a Ski and Snowboard Instructor Academy available for those interested in becoming a fully qualified and certified instructor. The course is very comprehensive and runs over a three-month period.

On-mountain bunk-style accommodation is available at a lodge operated by the Porter Heights Ski Club, a few minutes below the car park.

SKIING AND BOARDING

Beginners are well catered for at Porter Heights. From what I've observed during my visits there, the progression from the learner's area to the T-bars seems to happen very quickly. A learner's tow and platter lift down near the base area is a great place to start before progressing to the No. 1 T-bar. This area is well separated from the main runs and faster skiers and boarders, reducing the intimidation factor and risk of collisions.

Intermediates may wish to choose the one-kilometre-long cruising runs either side of the No. 1 T-bar. Here you can make short or wide turns on superbly groomed snow which is served well by additional snowmaking. From the top of the No. 3 T-bar you can traverse along the cat track Adrian's Highway, before dropping into McNulty's Basin and back to the main groomed runs of the No. 1 T-bar. In good snow conditions, stronger intermediates should observe the slope out to the right on your way up on the No. 3 T-bar. Here you will find a great spot to gain more confidence before having a go at the black diamond runs.

From Adrian's Highway advanced skiers and sliders can drop into Solitude and McNulty's Basin, or for those wanting a real rush Bluff Face is for you — a steep run of 38-degrees, not for the faint-hearted. My personal favourite is Big Mama, a huge run of 620 m vertical from the top of the No. 3 T-bar. The easiest way to access the run is to climb a short way above the T-bar and traverse across to the top of the slope — from here Big Mama waits. This is one of the longest, steepest runs in the Southern Hemisphere. I haven't seen many make it to the bottom non-stop (or in my case without eating snow!). This slope will really test the legs and heart of even the finest skiers and boarders.

The mountain is one huge play area for freestylers and boarders and the terrain park, with heaps of hits and bumps, rails and boxes, is a popular meeting place for the young.

Porter Heights has excellent back-country terrain such as Powder Bowl out over the ridge from Big Mama, and Crystal Valley over the Bluff Face ridge line. These runs are outside the ski area boundary so you must check in with ski patrol staff before heading out. In fact, if you are visiting for the first time and are unsure of which slopes to hit first, ask any of the staff or patrollers. They will point you in the right direction according to your ability.

HOW TO GET THERE

From Christchurch: Porter Heights is around an hour's drive by car and approximately 90 km from the airport. Take State Highway 73 through Darfield, Sheffield, Springfield and Porters Pass; the ski area turn-off is well signposted on the left. The well-maintained access road is an easy drive and chains should always be carried, though are seldom required.

Great:
For those who want to get maximum vertical for their dollar.

Not so great:
If you prefer chairs to T-bars.

FACILITIES

- 3 T-bars
- 1 poma
- 1 learner tow
- Snowmaking
- Groomers
- Terrain park
- Ski and snowboard rental
- Repairs and tuning shop
- Licensed café
- Ski and Snowboard School
- Alpine lodge accommodation (Porter Heights Ski Club

SEASON: JUNE–OCTOBER

Terrain Rating

Beginner	30%
Intermediate	30%
Advanced	40%

MT HUTT

ADDRESS

Mt Hutt, Methven, Canterbury
Telephone: (03) 302 8811; (03) 307 6315
Email: service@mthutt.co.nz Web: www.nzski.com

THE SKI AREA

Elevation: 2086 metres
Vertical descent: **683** metres
Skiable area: 365 hectares

Just over an hour from Christchurch and often one of the first ski areas to open each season, Mt Hutt is situated high in the Southern Alps overlooking the Canterbury Plains.

At an altitude of 2086 m, powder snow falls regularly into Mt Hutt's wide alpine basin. This, coupled with 42 ha of snowmaking, gives good snow cover on all runs for most of the season. The area is renowned amongst skiers and boarders at home and abroad for the quality and diversity of its terrain.

Base facilities at Mt Hutt are very good, featuring a brasserie, bar, caféteria, shop and rental area, ticketing, storage and a comprehensive medical centre. The area operates a very good children's centre and crèche, giving mums and dads plenty of time to themselves on the slopes.

Mt Hutt's 365 hectares of lift-accessed terrain is adequately served by three chairs, including a high-speed six-seater to the summit where many intermediate and advanced runs can be found. Beginners are transported by the magic carpet on a gentle slope outside the base area as well as a quad chair to the top of Exhibition and Broadway trails.

The snowsports school is well run with instructors of the highest standard for both skiers and boarders. Group lessons are almost two hours in duration and are reasonably priced. Private lessons are one hour in duration with the best deal, in my mind, being the Early Bird — this is a morning private session costing less than at peak times. A bonus too is that there are smaller lift queues in the mornings, so you tend to get more time skiing with the instructor than you usually would.

The Skiwi Pak for kids is a great deal where the children are looked after indoors in the crèche, plus they receive an hour's ski instruction during each morning and afternoon session.

SKIING AND BOARDING

Much of the intermediate and advanced terrain at Mt Hutt can be accessed from the top of the Summit Six Chair. Riding up on the chair you will get a clear view of the advanced runs High Dive and Virgin Mile, which you can get to by traversing along the ridge to your right — continue along this ridge to the Rakaia Saddle Chutes, pick a line and go for it. The Saddle Chutes are open when conditions permit and because the run ends below the lift line, a free shuttle service operates.

To the left riding up on the Summit Six you can see Fascination and the upper end of Hubers Run, two very good intermediate slopes that link up at the top of Broadway and on to the bottom lift station. Out further left are the Towers and the less-visible double diamond chutes of South Face, both great advanced skiing and boarding in powder conditions, but lethal when it's icy. Mt Hutt ski patrol staff continually monitor snow and weather conditions; when necessary they will close areas deemed unsafe.

Snowboarders and freeskiers are well catered for with two half pipes and a terrain park with plenty of bumps, jumps, hits, rails and tabletops. Features are constantly upgraded and the pipes kept in good condition with the aid of a pipe shaper.

From the Towers Triple Chair there are several great runs down Montezuma's Ridge and International to, if snow conditions permit, the bottom lift station. Should the lower section be closed, cut across to the left on your way down, just above car park level to the Towers' mid-loading station.

FACILITIES

- Chair lifts: 1 high-speed six-seater, 1 quad, 1 triple
- 1 magic carpet
- 42 snowmaking hectares
- Café
- Licensed restaurant
- Snow shop
- Equipment rental
- Children's centre and crèche
- Snowsports school
- Saddle Chutes Shuttle

HOW TO GET THERE

From Christchurch: Take State Highway 77 through Darfield and the Rakaia Gorge, go past the Methven turn-off and continue along SH 72 for another 5 km to the Mt Hutt road intersection on your right.

There is another route I often use; it's definitely quicker, especially at busy times. On SH 73 from Christchurch, around 10 km past West Melton, is a turn-off to Hororata. Follow it to Hororata, crossing several river fords, carry on through Hororata to meet the main highway near Windwhistle and turn left towards the Rakaia Gorge and on to SH 72 to the Mt Hutt turn-off.

From Methven. Take SH 77 north and follow the signs to Mt Hutt.

Mt Hutt's access road is a reasonably comfortable drive for all vehicles, apart from one exposed ridge section which can particularly affect campervans during high winds. In winter snow conditions it is advisable for vehicles to carry tyre chains.

Great:
Good variety of terrain. Usually reliable snow cover and a long season.

Not so great:
Can get crowded on weekends and school holidays.

SEASON: JUNE–OCTOBER

Terrain Rating

Beginner	25%
Intermediate	50%
Advanced	25%

MT HUTT
HELICOPTERS

ADDRESS

Mt Hutt Helicopters, 880 Forks Road, Alford Forest, Methven
Telephone: (03) 302 8401; 0800 443 547 Email: info@mthuttheli.co.nz
Web: www.mthuttheli.co.nz

THE SKI AREA

Operating from helipads at the Heli Centre in Alford Forest or up on the Mt Hutt ski area, Mt Hutt Helicopters offer a range of heli-ski and heli-board options to suit anyone from first timers to the most seasoned back-country helicopter addicts.

The Mt Hutt and Arrowsmith ranges provide perfect terrain with great powder snow and stunning views for skiers and snowboarders to savour, whether you choose one run or a full day of adrenalin-pumping vertical.

Mt Hutt Helicopters operates Squirrel and Hughes 500 machines. Their pilots are highly trained with many years of experience flying in New Zealand's unique mountain environment.

Alpine Guides, one of the country's most respected guiding companies, provide the personnel who will get you down the deep powder bowls, rolling valleys and steep chutes with maximum safety.

Group sizes are kept small and whenever possible graded according to ability. At the beginning of each heli day you will be briefed on all aspects of back-country mountain safety including the use of an avalanche transceiver.

North Peak Run is Mt Hutt Heli's most popular option. This run descends a large ungroomed basin offering 800 vertical metres of skiing or boarding north of the Mt Hutt ski area. Access is by helicopter from the ski area in guided parties. The North Park run is moderately priced and the perfect introduction to heli-skiing or heli-boarding.

Mt Hutt Back-country is a three-run package exploring some of the best terrain on the range. Your guide will help you to search out the best runs in an area well known for the amount of powder it gets. Book your flight at the Mt Hutt ski area car park.

The Arrowsmith Ranges have some of the best heli-skiing terrain in New Zealand with runs averaging 750–1200 vertical metres. Flying out of their helipad at Glenfalloch Station, Mt Hutt Helicopters can arrange complimentary transport from Methven to Glenfalloch or you can use your own vehicle. A day in the Arrowsmiths consists of five heli runs, guide services, safety equipment, a sumptuous lunch and transport to the helipad. After a safety briefing first groups fly in at around 10 a.m.; you will be back in Methven by 5 p.m. Extra runs are available for a charge.

Prices for all Mt Hutt Helicopters options are available on their website. For private charters or scenic flights give them a call or send the office an email.

Great:
For intermediate to experts, the variety of terrain and superb snow conditions.

Not so great:
For beginners

ADDRESS

Mt Potts Back-country, Mt Somers, Canterbury
Telephone: (03) 303 9060 lodge; (03) 303 9738 homestead
Email: mc@mtpotts.co.nz Web: www.mtpotts.co.nz

MT POTTS BACK-COUNTRY

NELSON/MARLBOROUGH & CANTERBURY

THE SKI AREA

Elevation: 2140 metres
Vertical descent: 740 metres
Skiable area: 320 hectares

Driving into Mt Potts past Lake Clearwater, you can be forgiven if the magnificent scenes unfolding before you at every turn distract somewhat from the gravel road ahead. I found it extremely difficult to focus on driving one sunny August afternoon, almost losing control as I approached the final bridge just before Mt Potts Lodge. My first word of advice is to pull over and stop if you want to take in this awesome panoramic view of the valley surrounded by a ring of majestic snow-capped mountains. Such beauty inspired film makers to shoot scenes for the *Lord of the Rings* film trilogy here.

Mt Potts is a boutique ski area, an hour's drive from Methven off State Highway 72, inland from Mt Somers village. Groups of a maximum of 14 people get to experience New Zealand's only heli-accessed snowcat skiing and snowboarding terrain. This is back-country in style!

With a high point of 2254 m, Mt Potts catches plenty of dry powder to satisfy those few fortunate skiers and boarders descending a variety of runs down the mountain's bowls, gullies and chutes to the snowcat waiting below.

The day starts at 8 a.m., with a helicopter ride up to the ski area. Following a safety briefing, which includes how to correctly use an avalanche transceiver, the snowcat takes your group up to the summit for a first run. Your experienced guides will show you the best and safest slopes to suit your ability. At around noon you'll take a break for lunch and then carry on skiing or boarding until 3.30 p.m. Save your legs for the last run — it's a whopping 2 km back to the helicopter for the flight back to Mt Potts Lodge.

Each day skiers and snowboarders will average 12–14 runs at Mt Potts or 18,000 vertical ft.

You can visit Mt Potts for the day or stay in the lodge. I recommend that you stay at least one night, preferably two, if you want to get the best out of a Mt Potts Back-country experience.

Mt Potts Lodge is a converted woolshed with shared or twin rooms and a cottage. All rooms have under-floor heating with linen and towels provided. Enjoy an excellent farm-style dinner in the licensed restaurant before settling back in the bar to relax around the pot belly stove and re-live your day on the snow. (Please note, bookings are essential.)

HOW TO GET THERE

From Christchurch and Methven: Drive along State Highway 77 through Darfield and across the Rakaia River bridge to the Methven turn-off. Drive straight through to SH 72 and carry on to Mt Somers, then turn right to Hakatere and Lake Clearwater. Mt Potts' access road runs through high-country farmland past the Lake Clearwater village. On a clear day this has to be one of the most scenic roads in New Zealand.

From Queenstown, Mt Cook and Lake Tekapo: Take SH 79 to Geraldine then turn left, just past the Orari Bridge, onto SH 72 to Mt Somers. At Mt Somers turn left to Hakatere and Lake Clearwater.

If you want to save valuable skiing or snowboarding time, Mt Potts can arrange private charter plane or helicopter flights to their own airstrip from almost anywhere in the South Island.

Great:
For those in search of their own private back-country powder domain.

Not so great:
For beginners or for those inexperienced in off-piste snow conditions.

FACILITIES

- Helicopter
- Snowcat
- Mt Potts Lodge accommodation
- Restaurant
- Bar

SEASON: ❄ JULY–SEPTEMBER

Terrain Rating

Beginner	0%
Intermediate	50%
Advanced	50%

MACKENZIE COUNTRY

The Mackenzie Basin is one of the most spectacular regions I have visited. On a clear day the majestic sight of Aoraki/Mt Cook surrounded by the snowy peaks of the Southern Alps truly is a sight to behold. The basin has plenty of accommodation in the towns of Fairlie, Tekapo, Mount Cook Village, Twizel, Omarama and Lake Ohau. A number of private individuals offer farmstay or homestay-style accommodation, something I can recommend to visitors wishing to mix with the locals or for those wanting a taste of life on a high-country farm.

Agriculture and outdoor pursuits are the mainstays of the local economy in this wilderness area. Activities such as climbing, trekking, skiing and boarding, heli-skiing, ice skating, trout or salmon fishing, mountain biking, boating, scenic flights, golf, horse treks, hunting and much more are all to be found within a short distance of the region's centres.

Located in close proximity to Mt Dobson, Fox Peak and Roundhill ski areas is the small farming town of Fairlie. You will find good accommodation at reasonable rates here together with several superb cafés and restaurants, a golf course, ski, snowboard and tyre-chain rental, a supermarket and a few shops.

Lake Tekapo township, situated right on the lake shore, has accommodation, shops and a number of booking offices for activities in the area. The Church of The Good Shepherd is a South Island icon and one of the most photographed buildings in New Zealand; you'll find it only a short distance from the main highway. Roundhill is the nearest ski area to Tekapo, a scenic drive of only a half hour or so along the eastern shores of the lake.

Mt Cook Village lies at the head of Lake Pukaki. It is a centre for much of the climbing, trekking, heli-skiing, Tasman Glacier skiing and mountain 'flightseeing' activities to be had in the Aoraki/Mount Cook region. The town has accommodation, from budget to luxury, an airport, and activities booking offices.

The towns of Twizel and Omarama have a good range of accommodation, and are also reasonably close to the Ohau ski area. If you are travelling in a campervan or are self-catering, Twizel has a small shopping centre where you can stock up on provisions. Lake Ohau has accommodation at the base of the ski area access road.

FOX
PEAK

❄

ADDRESS

Fox Peak Ski Area, Fairlie, South Canterbury
Telephone: (03) 685 8539 ski field; (03) 684 7358
Email: ski@foxpeak.co.nz **Web:** www.foxpeak.co.nz

THE SKI AREA

Elevation: 1850 metres
Vertical descent: **580 metres**
Skiable area: 350 hectares

Situated in the Two Thumb Range beneath the 2331-m summit of Fox Peak, this ski area offers a substantial amount of terrain. Skiers and snowboarders of all abilities will enjoy the large variety of runs and powder-filled bowls to be found on Fox Peak's sunny east-facing slopes.

Operated by the Fox Peak Ski Club, the area is serviced by four rope tows giving a total vertical of 580 m. For the fitness gurus who may wish to climb to the summit of Fox Peak, you will be rewarded with a massive vertical descent of 1100 m. On a powder day you will not find better skiing anywhere; in fact the Two Thumb Range is renowned for its heli-skiing territory, such is the quality of snow on these mountains.

Facilities on the area are basic. The car park is located very close to a public shelter and ticket office which sells snacks and drinks. There is no rental equipment available so make sure you hire your gear in the nearby town of Fairlie if needed.

Group ski and snowboard lessons are available as part of a ski week package run by the ski club. Private lessons at Fox Peak are excellent value. For better skiers and boarders' a private session can be a great way to improve your technique while exploring the area if you are visiting for the first time.

Accommodation is available 3 km down the mountain road at the ski club's Fox Lodge. A diesel generator supplies power to the backpacker-style lodge where your rates include meals. Guests are expected to assist club members with light duties. You will need to bring a sleeping bag, pillowcase, lunch, clothing, and so on. It pays to book ahead — especially after a fresh dump of snow.

SKIING AND BOARDING

Skid Row is a short rope tow next to the car park. Situated on a gentle slope, it is ideal for the kids or first-timers to get a feel for the snow. This is also a good tow to learn the art of using a nutcracker.

The Meadow Tow is great to even further develop those nutcracker skills. Beginners who have gained some confidence, as well as intermediates, will really enjoy cruising the runs either side of this lift. It covers a distance of 700 m on a wide groomed slope, superb for perfecting those carving turns.

Advanced and stronger intermediate skiers and riders can choose several more challenging runs from the Tasman Tow. Shirt Front down the tow line is a good one while the North Slope or Happy Valley are both fantastic in powder conditions.

Apex Tow transports patrons to the upper ridge and to some fantastic skiing and boarding in the South Basin. From the summit of Apex there's a top run descending the South Slope, finishing at the base area.

Fox Peak has excellent back-country terrain for the experienced. Always check with ski patrol before heading out, make sure you carry the correct equipment and do not ski out of bounds alone.

This ski area has huge future potential. There are plans to further improve facilities with the addition of T-bars to the area. Should this happen, it will open up a lot of new and exciting terrain. Watch this space.

FACILITIES

- 4 rope tows
- 1 groomer
- Shelter
- Canteen
- On-mountain accommodation

HOW TO GET THERE

From Christchurch: Take State Highway 79 through Geraldine. After a winding section of road a few kilometres prior to Fairlie you will reach the summit of a hill called Mt Michael. Turn right at an intersection next to The Farm Barn Café and continue through farmland and past Lake Opua to an intersection with Clayton Road. Turn right, continuing for around 10 minutes along Clayton Road to the ski area access road on your left.

From Queenstown: Take SH 8 through Omarama, Twizel, Tekapo and on to Fairlie. Turn onto SH 79 towards Geraldine and then turn left after 500 m on to Clayton Road. Stay on Clayton Road for 20 km until you reach the Fox Peak Ski Area sign on your left.

The access road is well maintained, though care should be taken. Always carry tyre chains.

Great:
Skiing or boarding with no crowds. If you just want to get away from it all.

Not so great:
If you don't like nutcracker tows.

SEASON: JULY–OCTOBER

Terrain Rating

Beginner	15%
Intermediate	65%
Advanced	20%

MT DOBSON SKI AREA

ADDRESS

Mt Dobson Ski Area, Fairlie
Telephone: (03) 685 8039
Email: mtdobson@xtra.co.nz **Web:** www.dobson.co.nz

THE SKI AREA

Elevation: 2110 metres
Base elevation: 1700 metres
Vertical descent: 415 metres
Skiable area: 400 hectares

Mt Dobson lies at the gateway to the Aoraki/Mt Cook region, not quite mid-way between Christchurch and Queenstown. The ski area is a leisurely 45-minute scenic drive from the nearby town of Fairlie on one of the easier mountain roads I've had to negotiate. The base area and car park is the highest in New Zealand at 1725 m.

Situated in a 3 km-wide south-easterly facing bowl, Mt Dobson gets some of the driest powder snow in the country. This southerly aspect also helps to keep the snow in good condition for long periods of time.

Base facilities are not of a big resort standard but they are quite adequate for the amount of people skiing and boarding on the area. The café, ski and board rental and ticketing are all adjacent to the car park.

A triple chairlift, T-bar and a platter disperse skiers and boarders efficiently over the mountain with very little queuing. Beginners to experts will be satisfied with the variety of terrain options from which to choose.

Snowboarders and twintippers will have a lot of fun on Mt Dobson — it is a natural terrain park with plenty of jumps, rails, kickers and a natural half pipe.

Ski School is a small personal operation offering group or private instruction for all ability levels. A race training programme operates on weekends and there are plenty of activities to keep the kids occupied during the school holidays.

SKIING AND BOARDING

The learner's slope can be found just above the parking area. Served by a rope tow and platter lift, this slope is one of the largest beginner areas in the country. It is the ideal place for budding skiers and snowboarders to gain a little confidence before moving on to Dobson's more challenging runs.

Intermediate riders and skiers have plenty of runs to choose from on either side of the triple chairlift or the T-bar. From the top of the chair you may take a fast line to your left down the FIS course to the loading station, or to your right is Flat Out, a really good run descending down through the West Valley. Over on the T-bar it's a little steep up top so take it easy, sideslip down if you wish to where you'll find the upper part of M1. M1 is always a good ride in any condition.

Advanced skiers and boarders will find access to more challenging runs from the East and West Trails. These trails traverse below the ridge line left and right from the T-bar summit. Out East and Shirt Front join up with M1 back to the T-bar loading station, while out west you can choose a line anywhere along the trail for a fast steep run down to the chairlift base area. If you enjoy moguls try Shirt Front.

Further out in the West Valley is some good semi-back-country terrain. You can get to these slopes by traversing across from the summit of the chairlift out wide of Easy Run. You will find great powder skiing and boarding after a storm on these slopes and they're usually the last to be tracked out, because a hike up to the access road may be required if you descend too low.

Snowboarders, freestylers or jibbers can drop into a natural half pipe found just below the FIS course. I've seen boarders occupy themselves for hours there with a number of hits, lips, kickers and jumps keeping them amused.

Mt Dobson is a family-owned and operated ski area. The owners take great pride in keeping a high standard of service and snow conditions, so they offer a warranty. If you are not happy with your day, weather or snow conditions, you can return your lift pass before 10.30 a.m. and they will give you a voucher for another day.

FACILITIES

- 1 triple chair
- 1 T-bar
- 1 learner platter Lift
- 1 beginner rope tow
- Ski and snowboard rental
- Caféteria
- Groomers
- Ski School
- Natural half pipe

HOW TO GET THERE

From Christchurch: The drive takes 184 km or 2¼ hours. Take State Highway 1 to Rangitata, then SH 79 through Geraldine to Fairlie. From Fairlie, SH 8 to the mountain access road is about 11 km. From there it is 15 km up to the ski area car park.

From Tekapo: Drive on SH 8 through Burke's Pass for 43 km or 30 minutes to the Mt Dobson access road on your left.

Bus transport is available from Fairlie at weekends and school holidays. Telephone 0800 487 287 or contact the ski area.

The Mt Dobson access road is a well-maintained gravel surface. It is an easy drive and suitable for all vehicles, including motorhomes. Chains should be carried as a precaution.

Great:
For all ability levels, superb learner's area, easy access from the road.

Not so great:
For nightlife. May not hold the expert's attention for too long.

SEASON: JUNE–OCTOBER

Terrain Rating

Beginner	25%
Intermediate	50%
Advanced	25%

ROUNDHILL SKI AREA

ADDRESS

Roundhill Ski Area, Lilybank Road, Lake Tekapo
Telephone: (03) 680 6977; (021) 680 694 (during season only)
Email: admin@roundhill.co.nz **Web:** www.roundhill.co.nz

THE SKI AREA

Elevation: 1600 metres
Base elevation: 1350 metres
Vertical descent: 250 metres
Skiable area: 100 hectares

The drive to Roundhill meanders alongside the idyllic shores of Lake Tekapo through high country farmland, surrounded by the majestic mountains of the Mt Cook region. On a clear winter's day, and there are plenty of those in the Mackenzie Country, I made the easy 10-minute drive up the access road from the lake shore to the ski area car park. At that moment of arrival, serious doubts came to me as to why I continue to live in the city. The panorama was stunning.

Roundhill, as the name suggests, is situated on a dome-shaped hill, the slopes of which are smooth and wide, providing an excellent playground for beginner and intermediate snowboarders and skiers. Extensive snowmaking and regular falls of dry natural snow provide an ideal surface over the whole area, which is groomed nightly.

Two lifts, one a T-bar of more than 1 Km in length, and a beginner's platter, disperse skiers and boarders without the queues associated with many of the larger ski areas.

Base facilities include ticketing, first aid, a restaurant, bar and rental department. Roundhill continually update their ski and snowboard rental equipment with the latest gear. The restaurant deck is a relaxing place for a break and to enjoy excellent food and superb coffee.

Qualified instructors operate out of the Roundhill Ski School. They offer both group and individual lessons to skiers and snowboarders of all ability levels — beginner to expert.

For the little ones and non-skiers, the smooth gentle slopes near the base area are ideal territory for tubing and tobogganing. If you can't bring your own sled these may be hired from the rental department.

SKIING AND BOARDING

You will not find big-mountain terrain, large vertical drop-offs, chutes and steep faces at Roundhill — it's just not that sort of area and doesn't ever claim to be. Advanced skiers and boarders may not have the terrain to extend themselves to the limits, but this is a very good area for better skiers who are getting back into the sport after a layoff, or for those who just plain enjoy wide open cruising.

Between the car park and beginner's platter is a large area for learners. With a wide gentle gradient, this is a great place to sit beside your car and observe the kids as they enjoy themselves in the snow.

From the top of the 1.2 km Garaventa T-bar, there is a fast run down the lift line named Speedway. Be aware of other skiers and boarders joining the trail on the way down. Out to your right on the way down is Karl's Way, a wide slope where long sweeping turns can be made with ease; it's a good run for intermediate and advanced skiers to perfect their technique. After a fresh snowfall, get on the slope early — Roundhill looks to be a great area to learn to ski powder.

Although not a terrain park enthusiast's dream, Roundhill has a number of features in the pipeline to amuse freestylers and twintippers. The open slopes here are a very good training ground for boarders to improve their downhill technique.

Roundhill is the ideal, almost perfect beginner and intermediate ski and snowboarding area; a great place to start the kids or for adults starting who are intimidated by steep slopes and large crowds. In good snow conditions the whole area is skiable by almost everyone, allowing families and groups of varying abilities to ski and board together.

SKI TEKAPO

www.roundhill.co.nz

FACILITIES

- 1 T-bar
- 1 beginner platter
- Snowmaking
- 2 groomers
- Ski and Snowboard School
- Ski and board rental
- Restaurant
- Bar

HOW TO GET THERE

From Christchurch: Take State Highway 1 to Rangitata, then SH 79 through Geraldine, Fairlie and Burkes Pass. As you descend a hill to the lake shore just before Tekapo township, turn off to the right into Lilybank Road. Continue along this road along the lake shore for around 20–25 minutes until you reach the Roundhill Ski Area access road. From the entrance to the car park is an 8 km road easily negotiated by campervans and buses.

From Queenstown: State Highway 8 passes through Omarama, Twizel and Lake Tekapo. On the north side of Tekapo as you leave the lake shore, turn left into Lilybank Road and follow the instructions as above.

Great:
For families. Superb beginner and intermediate cruising terrain.

Not so great:
For advanced skiers and boarders.

SEASON:
LATE JUNE-OCTOBER

Terrain Rating

Beginner	20%
Intermediate	80%
Advanced	0%

SKI THE TASMAN

ADDRESS

Ski the Tasman, Aoraki/Mt Cook Village
Telephone: (03) 435 1834 **Email:** mtcook@alpineguides.co.nz
Web: www.skithetasman.co.nz

THE SKI AREA

Located high in the Southern Alps below New Zealand's highest peak, skiing on the Tasman Glacier has been a favourite back-country adventure for over 40 years.

Alpine Guides, one of New Zealand's premier guiding companies, operates Ski the Tasman as an integral part of their winter programmes. Expert pilots with years of experience in New Zealand mountain flying operate a fleet of Cessna 185s and PC6 Pilatus Porter planes fitted with retractable skis.

During the cold winter months of July until September when powder snow is at its best, Ski the Tasman flies small groups of skiers, escorted by a professional mountain guide, to the head of the glacier. The Tasman Glacier is 27 km long with an average width of 1.6 km; an average run with Ski the Tasman will average 10 km through some of the most spectacular alpine scenery in the world.

A standard day starts at 9 a.m. with organising ski rentals and a safety briefing. Take off is at 10 a.m., depending on numbers, with the groups returning to Mt Cook Airport at around 3 p.m.

You do not have to be an expert to ski the Tasman. Anyone of an intermediate level will enjoy the experience of the glacier's moderate wide open slopes. Skiing on deep ungroomed snow is made a lot easier by using powder or fat skis. A lot wider than your standard carving skis, they make for effortless turns and glide with ease. If you do not own a pair it is worth renting them.

A Ski the Tasman trip begins with a 20-minute skiplane flight up New Zealand's longest glacier to a snow landing at 2400 m. After taking time to enjoy the views down the Murchison headwall and out to the West Coast, we ski on down to the Darwin Ice Fall where it is often possible to ski or hike through spectacular ice caves and seracs(isolated blocks ofice). Another half-hour of gentle skiing ends at Darwin Corner where the ski plane is waiting to take us back up for lunch. The 'Cornice Wall' lunch spot is well placed with expansive views down the glacier to Mt Cook and up to the looming ice cliffs of Hotchstetter Dome. From there the second run takes a different line down the glacier, and if conditions are good there is time to explore the maze of crevasses at 'Canyonlands' on the way back to the skiplane and the flight home.

HOW TO GET THERE

By road:

From Christchurch: It's 330 km or 3½–4 hours driving on State Highway 1 to Rangitata, then take SH 79 to Geraldine and Fairlie. From Fairlie turn on to SH 8 through Burkes Pass and Lake Tekapo. At Lake Pukaki turn right on to SH 80 and carry on for 56 km to Aoraki/Mt Cook Village.

From Queenstown: It's 270 km or around 3 hours by car on SH 8. Go through Omarama, Twizel and then turn left at Lake Pukaki on to SH 80 to Aoraki/Mt Cook.

By air:

Local airlines operate regular scheduled flights from Christchurch and Queenstown to Mt Cook Airport.

ADDRESS

Wilderness Heliskiing, Aoraki/Mt Cook Village,
Mt Cook National Park **Telephone:** (03) 435 1834
Email: mtcook@heliskiing.co.nz **Web:** www.heliskiing.co.nz

WILDERNESS HELISKIING

THE SKI AREA

Operated by Alpine Guides out of Aoraki/Mt Cook Village, Wilderness Heliskiing offers the best skiing and snowboarding in and around the Mt Cook National Park. It is the only company that can offer heli-skiing and boarding within the bounds of the park.

Situated in the heart of the Southern Alps amongst New Zealand's highest mountains, Wilderness Heliskiing take skiers and snowboarders to a vast selection of terrain, offering huge vertical descents, steep glaciers and rolling valleys. The season runs from July to October when cold winter powder snow is in its best condition.

A normal heli-skiing or heli-boarding day consists of five runs with an average vertical descent of 750–1200 m per run. Extra vertical may be provided depending on demand and conditions. When booking and arranging accommodation I recommend that you allow for a stay of two or three days in the area, just in case bad weather postpones operations.

Wilderness Heliskiing caters for clients of all ability levels, though I would suggest you will need a bit more than a wedge turn to enjoy heli-skiing.

Skiers and boarders are grouped according to their ability into groups of four, together with a highly experienced mountain guide. Each day begins with a full safety briefing, which includes the correct use of an avalanche transceiver.

Skiing powder snow these days has been made a lot easier since the introduction of wider 'fat' skis — these make turning in deep snow a breeze. Powder skis may be rented from Alpine Guides' booking office; snowboards are not available for hire so bring your own.

Runs vary from mellow bowls through to steep couloirs (gorges) and ice falls with a little of everything in between. Wilderness Heliskiing's landing sites are generally higher than other areas, providing longer runs and colder snow.

Nuns Veil Glacier is one of the classics. Expansive views from the 2500-metre landing site overlook the Mackenzie Basin to Aoraki/Mt Cook and the main peaks of the main divide, through Copeland Pass to the West Coast.

The run itself descends 1200 m, the first half a cruise down rolling terrain which steepens, narrowing to a squeeze past an ice cliff at the snout of the glacier. From here on the run opens out into a wide shaded gulley for another 600 metres of powder to your helicopter waiting on the valley floor.

HOW TO GET THERE

By road:

From Christchurch: After 330 km or 3 ½–4 hours driving on State Highway 1 to Rangitata, turn SH 79 to Geraldine and Fairlie. From Fairlie turn on to SH 8 through Burkes Pass and Lake Tekapo. At Lake Pukaki turn right on to SH 80 and carry on for 56 km to Aoraki/Mt Cook Village.

From Queenstown: It's 270 km or around 3 hours by car on SH 8. Go through Omarama, Twizel and then turn left at Lake Pukaki on to SH 80 to Aoraki/Mt Cook.

By air:

Local airlines operate regular scheduled flights from Christchurch and Queenstown to Mt Cook Airport.

Great:
For intrepid heli-ski or heli-board enthusiasts, strong intermediate to expert skiers and riders, and keen powder-hounds.

Not so great:
For beginners or nervous flyers.

SEASON:
JUNE–OCTOBER

Terrain Rating

Beginner	0%
Intermediate	40%
Advanced	60%

OHAU
SNOW FIELDS

ADDRESS

Lake Ohau, Mackenzie Country **Telephone:** (03) 438 9885
Email: mike.louise@ohau.co.nz
Web: www.ohau.co.nz

THE SKI AREA

Elevation: 1825 metres
Base elevation: 1425 metres
Vertical descent: 400 metres
Skiable area: 600 hectares

Only a short drive from the main highway between Christchurch and Queenstown, Lake Ohau, in the South Island's Mackenzie Country, is one of my favourite places to visit. Standing on an idyllic lake shore surrounded by the snow-capped mountains of the Southern Alps, the rest of the world and its problems seem like they're a million miles away.

The ski area road winds its way up from the Lake Ohau lodge situated on the lake shore to the car park, from which you will be rewarded with a magnificent panoramic view. Only a very short walk is required to the base facilities, which have everything needed for a comfortable day on the snow.

Lake Ohau's cosy day lodge is warmed inside by a wood fire while outside patrons take in spectacular views from the sundeck. Great food and coffee is served from the café.

Visitors can hire up-to-date ski and snowboard equipment from the rental department before registering for a lesson with Ohau's snow school. The instructors at Ohau are of an excellent standard, catering for skiers and snowboarders of any ability level. The school offers a very good starter's package: it includes a learner's lift ticket, instruction and ski or snowboard equipment.

Do not be fooled by a seeming lack of lift facilities. Ohau's double chair carries patrons almost to the top of Ridge Run with little in the way of a queue while a platter and learner tow takes care of those new to the snow.

SKIING AND BOARDING

Intermediate skiers and riders are treated to some very good runs on either side of the chairlift, a couple of favourites being The Towers and Shirt Front. Both of these runs are great in the fresh powder often found at Ohau. Riding the chair, you can pick some lines out to your left on a slope named Sun Run, where first tracks can often be made if you are there soon after a fresh snowfall.

When descending a line down The Towers, a good alternative is to cut across under the lift line at around half way and drop into Luge. Here you will find a good challenging run for advanced intermediate skiers and boarders, a good training ground before moving on to steeper terrain.

For the more advanced there is a steep face out to your right riding up; Exhibition and Escalator are two very good lines to show off your carving skills before descending to the T-bar loading station. If you are feeling energetic you could hike to the ridge summit above the T-bar. From here you will be treated to a descent in excess of 400 vertical metres to the base area — not bad for one T-bar ride.

Beginners who have gained confidence in their skiing and boarding ability will find groomed trails off the chairlift quite manageable. Boulevard is the easiest of these and runs the full length of the chair.

Parents can relax from the day lodge sundeck while watching their children progress during a lesson on the gentle slope of the beginners' area, or they may wish to assist them in learning to ride the easy-to-use fixed-grip tow near the café building.

I can highly recommend a stopover at Ohau Snow Fields if you are travelling north or south. Should you need accommodation for the night, Lake Ohau Lodge at the base of the access road is a great place to stay.

FACILITIES

- 1 double chair
- 1 platter Lift
- 1 fixed-grip beginner tow
- Ski and board rental
- Snow school
- Café
- Day lodge
- Souvenir shop
- Groomers
- Accommodation

HOW TO GET THERE

From Christchurch: Ohau is 320 km or 3½–4 hours driving. Take State Highway 8 through Fairlie, Tekapo and Twizel. The turn-off to Ohau is mid-way between Twizel and Omarama. Lake Ohau Lodge is 42 km from Twizel and Omarama, the ski area another 10 km along a well-kept gravel access road.

From Queenstown/Wanaka: Take SH 8 through Omarama and turn off left to Ohau, around halfway between Omarama and Twizel. From there follow the instructions above.

Great:
For intermediate skiers and boarders or for a stopover while travelling north or south.

Not so great:
For boarders wanting terrain parks or for those in search of night life.

SEASON:
JULY–OCTOBER

Terrain Rating

Beginner	20%
Intermediate	50%
Advanced	30%

Between the lakeside town of Wanaka and the holiday resort of Queenstown are arguably some of the best sking and snowboarding areas in the Southern Hemisphere. Here you have a selection of six skiing and boarding areas and a vast range of heli-ski terrain which is unrivalled in Australasia.

In both Wanaka and Queenstown there are many options to choose from as far as accommodation is concerned, with backpacker lodges, hotel or motels and camping grounds. It pays to shop around for prices though, as they tend to vary according to the time of year and whether the ski season is going well or not. If it's a lean snow year or tourism numbers are down there can often be good accommodation deals going.

If you are travelling on a tight budget there can be good prices at some of the various homestays and farmstays in the Southern Lakes area. Smaller towns nearby are also worth considering; these include Arrowtown, Cromwell and Alexandra.

There are plenty of activities in the Southern Lakes region including bungy jumping, white-water rafting, climbing, trekking, golf, paragliding, ice skating, lake cruises, jet boating, wine trails, off-road 4WD tours, scenic flights and mountain biking, to name a few. A worthwhile trip I can recommend from Queenstown is an excursion to Milford Sound. If you do book with one of the local tour operators make sure you add on the Milford Sound boat cruise. This cruise takes you through the sound past Mitre Peak to the Tasman Sea. It is a very spectacular trip even on a misty day — well worth the extra expense.

Wanaka has a small shopping centre near the lake where there are a number of cafés, bars, restaurants and takeaway food outlets. In town you will also find convenience food stores, ski/snowboard rental and retail shops and several mountain transport or heli-ski booking agents. If it's a wet day on the mountain a fun trip for the family is to visit the Warbirds Museum out at Wanaka Airport. Restored planes of the past, including Spitfires and Mustangs, are on display here, the site of the annual 'Warbirds Over Wanaka' airshow every Easter.

From Wanaka to the ski/boarding areas in the Cardrona Valley is a drive of only 15 minutes. To Treble Cone it is a comfortable trip around Lake Wanaka of around 35 minutes.

Queenstown is a busy resort town busting at the seams. There are heaps of shops to satisfy the most seasoned retail therapists, a wide variety of restaurants, cafés and bars and almost too many ski shops. Parking hasn't kept in pace with development so it can be difficult at times. Try to avoid the centre of town on a wet day, when thousands of skiers and boarders descend on the place in an effort to occupy themselves.

If you want something a little different, one of the more popular excursions is a Lake Wakatipu cruise on the historic steamship TSS *Earnslaw*. One of the most exciting boat rides I've ever experienced is the Shotover Jet, located at Arthurs Point. If you get the chance try it for yourself — you will not be disappointed. The Kawarau Jet is another good ride, which departs from the pier in central Queenstown.

TREBLE CONE

ADDRESS

Treble Cone, Wanaka
Telephone: (03) 443 7443 Email: tcinfo@treblecone.com
Web: www.treblecone.com

THE SKI AREA

Elevation: 2088 metres
Base elevation: 1255 metres
Vertical descent: 705 metres
Skiable area: 550 hectare

Treble Cone is situated high in the Southern Alps overlooking Lake Wanaka. The area has some of the best skiing and boarding in the Southern Lakes region, together with one of New Zealand's great alpine views.

Claiming to be the largest ski area in the South Island with the highest vertical, Treble Cone gets great powder days and has some of the best big-mountain freeskiing terrain in the south. Beginner and intermediate trails are groomed nightly while 50 hectares of snowmaking ensures adequate snow cover, especially early and late in the season. The longest intermediate run is over four Km long.

Arriving in the car park after negotiating the steep but well-maintained access road brings you close to the base area, where you will find the ticketing office, café, restaurant and bar. I have found that the coffee is great and the food superb. The main building also houses equipment rental, a ski and board workshop and the nearby beginner's area.

Treble Cone's ski and snowboard school is operated very professionally with a range of options for beginners to experts.

Something I would like to try next time I visit Treble Cone is their back-country touring experience. In this skiers and boarders are taught how to analyse terrain and avalanche hazards, and correctly use an avalanche transceiver. The instructor will also teach the correct techniques needed to get up and down the slopes of the back-country safely and efficiently.

The children's programme looks to be very comprehensive and offers instruction to kids from the age of three. An indoor childcare centre is available for children over three years of age or under three if accompanied by a parent.

SKIING AND BOARDING

A magic carpet and a platter lift for beginners are situated near the base area buildings. This is a great place to get started before heading up on the six-seater Land Rover Express chair from where several groomed trails — Triple Treat, Kea's Crossing and Nice & Easy — may be accessed.

Intermediate and advanced skiers and boarders have 90 percent of the terrain at their disposal, either off both sides of the Land Rover Express or over in the Saddle Basin, which is served by two chairs and a T-bar.

Looking down the mountain from the top of the six-seater, you will find the intermediate runs of Expressway and Mainstreet off to your left. Mainstreet is good intermediate cruising and a fun way to start the day. Over to the right, Side Winder follows down through a valley and links on to Rock Garden and Drainpipe — this is challenging intermediate stuff and popular with boarders.

The Main Basin has excellent advanced terrain with Gun Barrel being a favourite among the speedsters, as are several chutes near the summit. At times you will see adventurous skiers and boarders taking a line down one of these chutes and using the saddle track to launch themselves into Powder Bowl.

Treble Cone added a new quad chair to Saddle Basin during 2005, which opened up a good deal of new intermediate and advanced terrain, including Motatapu Chutes, a controlled back-country area where avalanche transceivers must be carried. Advanced skiers and boarders only are allowed into this area. The gates are closed during avalanche control work and reopen when safe conditions allow.

The South Ridge and Cloud Nine are very good intermediate runs either side of the Saddle Quad, while Mine Shaft and Payback are adrenalin rushes for experts down both sides of the same lift.

Snowboarders and freestylers can drop into a run named Super-Pipe by traversing from the top of the Saddle quad chair along Upper High Street. This run winds down through a snow-filled gully and forms one of the best natural pipes around. Treble Cone's terrain park is out to the right as you ride up on the Saddle double chair.

My experiences of skiing at Treble Cone have always been good ones — in good snow conditions better skiing and boarding would be hard to find.

FACILITIES

- Chairs: 1 six-seater, 1 quad, 1 double
- 1 T-bar
- 1 race-training T-bar
- 1 beginner platter lift
- 1 magic carpet
- Snowmaking
- Snow groomers
- Café
- Bar
- Retail shop
- Ski and board rental
- Workshop and tuning
- Ski and snowboard school
- Back-country tours
- Childcare centre
- Summer mountain biking and walking trails

HOW TO GET THERE

From Wanaka: It's a 35–40 minute drive on sealed road around the lake to the base of the mountain access road. From there it is 7 km of well-maintained gravel road to the car park. It is a steep but not too scary drive that can be negotiated by most vehicles, but always carry tyre chains just to be safe.

From Queenstown: It is around a one-and-a-half-hour drive and you can choose from two routes. You can either take State Highway 6 around the Pisa Range via Cromwell and Luggate to Wanaka, or in good driving conditions take the Crown Range Road through Cardrona. The Crown Range drive is quicker but do be very careful of icy patches, especially during early morning or later in the evening.

Shuttle services operate daily from Wanaka and Queenstown — contact Treble Cone for further information.

Great:
On its day, some of the best advanced skiing and snowboarding to be found anywhere.

Not so great:
Doesn't have a large variety of beginner terrain.

SEASON: JUNE–OCTOBER

Terrain Rating

Beginner	10%
Intermediate	40%
Advanced	50%

SNOW FARM

ADDRESS

Snow Farm, Cardrona Valley Road, Wanaka
Telephone: (03) 443 0300 Email: info@snowfarmnz.com
Web: www.snowfarmnz.com

THE SKI AREA

Elevation: 1980 metres
Base elevation: 1500 metres

Situated in the Pisa Range on the opposite side of the valley from Cardrona Ski Area between Wanaka and Queenstown, Snow Farm is the only dedicated cross-country ski area in New Zealand and arguably the best in the Southern Hemisphere.

Snow Farm caters for classic and skate techniques with over 50 km of superbly groomed trails, enough to suit people of all ages and ability levels. Visitors are welcome for the day or to stay in the lodge for a night or two. Maybe take up a weekly package, which includes accommodation, meals and instruction. For something a little different you may wish to try night skiing before dinner.

The Alpine Lodge is very comfortable, offering on-snow accommodation with magnificent views of the surrounding mountains. Guests have all the amenities required to make for a relaxing holiday. Enjoy brunch from the Verandah Café, or dinner in Snow Farm's fully licensed restaurant followed by a few drinks in the bar. Alpine Lodge patrons have the use of a gym, TV room and library.

Snow Farm offers a variety of instruction options to suit beginners through to advanced skiers. The introductory package is a good deal for the beginner. One of the area's ski school staff will help you to select the correct gear, teach you how to get back on your feet when you fall and how to walk and ski in the classic tracks.

The season begins at Snow Farm as soon as snow permits and continues through to October. Many international cross-country ski teams use the area for training during their off-season, a testimony in itself to Snow Farm's high standard of service and facilities.

Staff members in all areas of the operation are well informed, helpful and very pleasant. Snow Farm offers other activities including a supervised Tubing Park where you can hire a sled or tube and helmet by the hour. It's great fun for the kids, mum and dad.

SOUTHERN LAKES DISTRICT

Snow shoeing is an unusual sport in New Zealand; however it is a great way to explore Snow Farm's back-country areas. Bob Lee Hut and Meadow Hut are worth the trek for a night's stay. Both huts are stocked with wood, water and gas cookers. You will need to pack a sleeping bag, food and perhaps a drink or two!

CROSS-COUNTRY SKIING

My visit to Snow Farm coincided with one of the worst snow seasons on record — but all things considered, snow cover on the area's trails was pretty good, due in the main to snowmaking and some excellent work by the grooming staff.

Cross-country skiing is quite different from the downhill stuff I'm used to so I pulled out Snow Farm's product directory for an explanation as to what it's all about.

Classic skiing requires the least amount of physical conditioning and is most enjoyable at a beginner level. It involves making one central motion in the grooves on the trails.

Skate skiing is more like ice skating but with skis on wider groomed trails. Packed trails allow for a tremendous increase in glide and range of motion.

Cross-country skiing suits all ages and abilities. Athletes in other sports such as swimming, rowing, triathlon, multi-sport and mountain biking use cross-country skiing as off-season training, as it provides an entire body work out. Downhill skiers and snowboarders also find cross-country skiing of benefit as it will increase balance and precision.

Snow Farm's trail map shows a lot of beginner trails close to the Alpine Lodge area, and while intermediate and advanced trails start in close to the lodge and progress further out into the surrounding hills.

FACILITIES

- 50 km of trails
- Skate or classic
- Groomers
- Ski school
- Winter Sports Academy
- Tubing park
- Snow shoeing
- Rental equipment
- Shop
- Café
- Bar
- Licensed restaurant
- Ski In Ski Out Lodge accommodation

HOW TO GET THERE

From Queenstown: Take the Cardrona Valley Road State Highway 89 over the Crown Range. The turn-off to Snow Farm and Snow Park is on the right, a short distance past the historic Cardrona Hotel.

From Wanaka: Take the Cardrona Valley Road (SH 89) for around 35 minutes. The turn-off to Snow Farm is on your left almost opposite the Cardrona Ski Area access road.

Great:

For people who want sport in the snow without all the stuff that goes with downhill — the rope tows, the chairlifts, the possibility of broken bones, etc.

Not so great:

If you only enjoy downhill.

SEASON: JUNE–OCTOBER

Terrain Rating

Beginner	40%
Intermediate	40%
Advanced	20%

SNOW PARK

ADDRESS

Snow Park NZ, Crown Range, Cardrona Valley Road, Wanaka
Telephone: (03) 443 0333 Email: info@snowparknz.com
Web: www.snowparknz.com

THE SKI AREA

Elevation: 1530 metres
Vertical descent: 125 metres
Skiable area: 60 hectares

Located high in the Pisa Range overlooking Cardrona Valley, Snow Park is regarded as the ultimate area for park riders and is the best freestyle resort south of the equator.

Freestyle aficionados will find every possible terrain park feature you can imagine with over 40 rails, boxes, hits, jumps and pipes. Should you be a beginner to park riding or a competitive freestyle skier or snowboarder, there is something at Snow Park to suit everyone.

Snow Park is for the young or young at heart. Obviously targeting the younger skier or boarder, I was surprised to see a number of 'older' freestylers pulling off some very impressive manoeuvres to the applause and encouragement of nearby young ones, often with comments such as, "Are you OK, Dad?"

A hugely powerful music system pumps out sounds over the entire area while great food, coffee or beverages are served at the café overlooking the park.

Snow Park's impressive battery of snowguns operates each night to ensure maximum snow cover. All trails, features and pipes are groomed to perfection, providing a superb skiing or riding surface.

Snow Park offers custom coaching camps that are designed to suit individual needs. They even have a camp specifically set up for girls to get the most out of their riding experience.

Patrons are transported to the summit of the area on a fixed quad chairlift, at which point all of the terrain park features and runs may be accessed. For parents who are not freestyle types but may wish to bring their children to Snow Park for a different experience, you can cruise the slopes around the chairlift perfecting your carving technique while the kids have a ball elsewhere.

SOUTHERN LAKES DISTRICT

If you are a terrain park enthusiast visiting the Southern Lakes area, Snow Park is a must-do. Mums and dads, the kids will do the dishes and wash your car for months (well, maybe days!) should you treat them to a day or two at Snow Park.

HOW TO GET THERE

From Queenstown: Take and the Cardrona Valley Road (State Highway 89) over the Crown Range. The turn-off to Snow Park and Snow Farm is on the right, a short distance past the historic Cardrona Hotel.

From Wanaka: Take the Cardrona Valley Road (SH 89) for around 35 minutes. The turn-off to Snow Park is on your left almost opposite the Cardrona Ski Area access road.

FACILITIES

- 1 quad chair
- 1 super pipe
- 1 quarter pipe
- 1 camp pipe
- 40+ rails and boxes
- 15–25 rollers, hits and bumps
- Hips, spines and wall rides
- Beginner pipe, jumps and boxes
- Snowmaking
- Café
- Bar
- 5000-watt public stereo system
- Snow groomers
- Pipe shaper
- Skier X course
- Retail store
- Accommodation on-site

SEASON: JUNE–OCTOBER

Terrain Rating

Beginner	10%
Intermediate	45%
Advanced	45%

Great:
For snowboarders, freestyle skiers and terrain park enthusiasts.

Not so great:
For downhill and big mountain skiing or snowboarding.

CARDRONA
ALPINE RESORT

ADDRESS

Cardrona Alpine Resort, Cardrona Valley Road, Wanaka
Telephone: (03) 443 7341 Email: info@cardrona.com
Web: www.cardrona.com

THE SKI AREA

Elevation: 1894 metres
Vertical descent: 390 metres
Skiable area: 320 hectares

Situated between Queenstown and Wanaka, the Cardrona Alpine Resort offers some great skiing and riding, both on or off trail. Because of Cardrona's location high in the Crown Range it tends to be colder and gets regular dumps of dry powder.

Here you will find large amounts of wide open beginner and intermediate terrain, great free skiing and snowboarding facilities, and some very good advanced runs. If you are an intermediate this is the place for you.

Base facilities are of a high standard and include a licensed café, noodle bar, restaurant and a fantastic pizzeria over in Captain's Basin (I can personally recommend it!). The children's alpine centre, one of New Zealand's best, is a favourite with the kids and offers a variety of options from daycare only through to full ski and boarding programmes.

The development centre offers group or private skiing and snowboarding instruction together with a range of workshops encompassing telemark, freeski, freestyle, snowboard camps, and ski/snowboard instructor training. Instructors are of a very high standard and go out of their way to ensure that their students get maximum enjoyment while improving their technique.

Few New Zealand commercial ski areas have on-mountain accommodation. Cardrona has 10 apartment units with their own catering facilities, only a minute or two from the lifts.

SKIING AND BOARDING

Popular among snowboarders and freestyle skiers for the variety of terrain park facilities, Cardrona has hosted a number of national and international events.

The pipe park features four halfpipes — the International, Rookie, Moro Monster and Johnny Superpipe. Two pipes are usually opened on a daily rotational basis; as

temperatures warm they may close during the middle of the day to allow for reshaping.

Cardrona claims to have New Zealand's longest terrain park with two trails that run the length of the Whitestar Express chair. Heavy Metal trail is suited to advanced riders with jib features of up to 8 m while the Playzone trail has much smaller features.

Complementing the pipe and terrain parks is a Gravity Cross course of 800 m in length with plenty of curves and bumps to test the skills of race competitors.

Wide trails are a feature at Cardrona and the runs either side of McDougall's quad chair are a really good place to get started, especially for children or those gaining the confidence to tackle steeper terrain.

For intermediate skiers and boarders there are some cruisy runs down the lift line of the Whitestar Express chair, from which you will see the Heavy Metal and Playzone terrain parks out to the left on your way back up.

In good snow conditions, advanced skiers and riders can drop into Arcadia Chutes from the top of the Whitestar Express for some great runs down to the Comeback Trail. If you lack the confidence to tackle the chutes try Scum Valley, then cut across to the right into Powder Keg and Comeback.

Over in Captain's Basin, the Captain's quad chair has some very good intermediate runs such as Eagle Rock and Highway 89 and a couple of challenging advanced runs out right, down Secret Chute or Tulips.

PIPE SPECS

- Johnny Superpipe — 16 degrees, 5 m wall, 130 m long

- Moro Monster — 17 degrees, 5m wall, 100 m long

- International — 14 degrees, 3 m wall, 110 m long

- Rookie — 14 degrees, 3.5 m wall, 90 m long

SEASON: JUNE–OCTOBER

Terrain Rating

Beginner	25%
Intermediate	55%
Advanced	20%

FACILITIES

- Chair Lifts: 2 quad, 1 quad express
- 3 Magic Learner Lifts
- 1 platter lift
- Terrain parks
- Pipe park
- Gravity cross course
- Licensed café
- Bar
- Licensed restaurant
- Noodle bar
- Juice/coffee bar
- Captain's Basin Pizzeria
- Snow shop
- Ski and Snowboard School
- Rental equipment
- Ski and board workshop
- Medical centre
- Children's alpine centre
- On-field accommodation

HOW TO GET THERE

By Road

From Wanaka: The ski area is 34 km or just over half an hour in normal driving conditions. Take the Cardrona Valley Road, which lies between the Crown and Pisa mountain ranges; the ski area access road entrance is to your right, just prior to the historic Cardrona Hotel.

From Queenstown: Take State Highway 6A to Frankton, then SH 6 for about 12 km to the Crown Range, then turn off to Wanaka and Cardrona. The ski area entrance is on the left past the Cardrona Hotel. Total driving time from Queenstown is around 60 minutes in good conditions (58 km).

Be very careful when negotiating the Crown Range road during winter as ice and or snow can be a hazard. Always carry chains and check road conditions before travelling, especially during poor weather.

By Air

Air New Zealand has flights into Wanaka Airport from Christchurch, while a number of airlines fly to Queenstown.

Great:
Really good facilities, excellent beginner and intermediate terrain.

Not so great:
Experts may tire of it after a day or two.

CORONET PEAK

ADDRESS

Coronet Peak, Queenstown **Telephone:** (03) 442 4640
Email: service@coronetpeak.co.nz
Web: www.nzski.com

THE SKI AREA

Elevation: 1649 metres
Vertical descent: 420 metres
Skiable area: 280 hectares

Developed as the South Island's first resort-style ski area by Rudolph Wrigley and Sons during the 1940s, Coronet Peak is one of New Zealand's most popular commercial ski and snowboarding destinations. A good deal of this popularity is due to its close proximity to the nightlife, accommodation and activities in and around Queenstown, an easy mountain access road and superb on-mountain facilities.

When the snow is good at Coronet it's hard to beat, offering a variety of terrain from the gentle novice slope of Big Easy to more challenging lines such as the Back Bowls or Exchange Drop.

Lifts and facilities have been added progressively over the years with the latest addition being the Greengates Express Chair — a high-speed six-seater. State-of - the-art-top-to-bottom snowmaking has extended the season for Coronet, especially during lean snow years.

I found the ski and boarding school to be a smooth and professional operation. Most importantly, time is taken to ensure students are correctly graded into classes according to their ability. An international band of instructors are super friendly, knowledgeable and easy to understand. Group lessons are very good value and a great way to meet people,

Base facilities have everything you would expect of a well-established commercial area, including a very good restaurant and bar opening on to a huge sundeck, ski and snowboard rental, a ski shop, medical centre and guest services.

Skiwiland Crèche caters for children from the age of two. It's a great place for parents to leave their kids in a safe, fun-filled environment while they get in some time on the snow.

SKIING AND BOARDING

Coronet Peak has a large variety of intermediate terrain and is a great place to progress to more difficult and challenging runs. Reaching the summit of Coronet's Express Chair and moving off to your right leads on to Express Way, Donkey Serenade and Sugar's Run, or for the advanced intermediate why not try a steeper line down Arnold's Way? M1 and Shirt Front are both ideal runs to perfect those carving turns down to the base area.

Coronet's half pipe is immaculately shaped and groomed to FIS specifications. It is located close to the terrain park, where you will find a number of rails, boxes, ledges, hits and jumps. Both are popular hangouts for boarders and freestyle skiers.

Advanced skiers and snowboarders will find a good fast run down Pro-Am on the Coronet Express Chair. In good snow conditions Exchange Drop can be a challenge for some steeper turns down to the base of Rockey Gulley T-bar. A friend and I managed to find a good powder run (it was actually courtesy of windblown snowmaking that day) down the left side of the T-bar lift line. We skied this for a while until everyone else moved in when they saw the fun we were having.

The Meadows chair and a magic carpet provide access to very good novice terrain down Big Easy or to the bottom of M1.

For something really different give the night skiing and riding a go. Coronet Peak's floodlit main runs are lit on Friday and Saturday nights until 9pm from mid-July until September.

HOW TO GET THERE

From Queenstown: Take Gorge Road Road to Arthur's Point. After crossing the bridge just past the Arthur's Point Pub, head up the hill past the camping ground. A couple of kilometres further on your left is the turnoff to Coronet Peak. The total driving time is around 25 minutes (18 km).

From Wanaka: Drive to Luggate, then take State Highway 6 past Cromwell and through the Kawarau River Gorge (beware of ice during winter), then turn off to Arrowtown near Lake Hayes. Coronet Peak is well signposted through Arrowtown and a few kilometres past the Millbrook Resort entrance.

An alternate route from Wanaka is over the Crown Range past Cardrona, Snow Park and Snow Farm ski areas. This is a wonderful drive provided you check the road conditions, especially during or after a snow storm. The historic Cardrona Hotel, about halfway through the valley, is well worth a visit for a rest and refreshments.

Shuttle services run regularly from Queenstown. Contact the Queenstown Snow Centre, (03) 442 4640, for details and schedules.

Great:
For skiers and riders of all ability levels, for families and it's very close to Queenstown.

Not so great:
Coronet's lower altitude can suffer from a lack of natural snow at times; the man-made snow here is not too bad though.

FACILITIES

- Chair Lifts: 1 high-speed six-seater, 1 Express Quad, 1 double
- 1 T-bar
- 1 beginner handle tow
- 1 magic carpet
- Terrain park
- Half pipe
- Café
- Bar
- Restaurant
- Snowmaking
- Ski shop
- Ski and snowboard rental
- Ski and snowboard school
- Snow groomers
- Night skiing (Friday and Saturdays, July–Sept)
- Crèche

SEASON: JUNE–OCTOBER

Terrain Rating

Beginner	20%
Intermediate	45%
Advanced	35%

SOUTHERN LAKES DISTRICT

THE REMARKABLES

ADDRESS

The Remarkables, Queenstown
Telephone: (03) 4424615
Email: service@theremarkables.co.nz Web: www.nzski.com

THE SKI AREA

Elevation: 1943 metres
Vertical descent: **357** metres
Skiable area: 220 hectares

Developed in a mountain range of the same name above Lake Wakatipu, The Remarkables' higher altitude and sheltered basin locality means more natural snow and less need for snowmaking. The area is close to Queenstown and complements nearby Coronet Peak by easing weekend crowds and offering a contrast in terrain.

Some great off-piste slopes will challenge adventurous freeriders, skiers and snowboarders, while the excellent beginner terrain and facilities encourage development of the less experienced.

The Ozone Tubing Park is a fun place for the kids (and me!) and if you get the opportunity, take a ride on the Shadow Basin chair, at the top of which is a lookout with breathtaking views of Lake Wakatipu, Queenstown and surrounding mountain ranges. Do not forget your camera.

On-mountain facilities are excellent and include a licensed café, children's centre and crèche. I found the restaurant service and the food quality to be of a high standard.

SKIING AND BOARDING

Experienced skiers and riders will find some very good runs off both sides of the Shadow Basin chair. The longest run, Homeward Bound (1.5 km), takes you below the base area to the mountain access road; a regular shuttle will transport you back to the lifts. In good snow conditions Alta Chutes and Boulder Basin are great runs, as are those off Anzac Trail, to the right of the Sugar Bowl Chair.

The Sugar Bowl Chair offers good intermediate terrain with Water Race, Fall Line and Cross Fall and some challenging runs on the top half of Shadow Basin. Confident intermediates may wish to try Homeward Bound in good snow conditions.

Riders and freestylers enjoy hanging out to music at the regularly maintained Terrain Park and Superpipe, and getting some great runs by dropping into chutes such as Doolans, Gallipoli and those above Lake Alta, to name just a few.

New people to the sport may wish to start on the handle tow at the base area before progressing to the Alta Chair. Here you will find some confidence-building runs out left down Alta Green or Turquoise before moving on to the groomed trails of Sugar Bowl.

The Snowsports School has some great lesson packages for beginners, which include lessons, lift pass and rental equipment. During the lesson I undertook, our instructor

FACILITIES

- Chairs, 3 quads
- 1 magic carpet
- 1 beginner handle tow
- Terrain park
- Super pipe
- Tubing park
- Snowmaking
- Snowsports School
- Groomers
- Licensed café
- Shop
- Ski and board rental
- Crèche

imparted knowledge easily and communicated well with the group. It was pleasing to observe that every endeavour is made to place students into their correct ability group. The group lesson of 1 hour 50 minutes is extremely good value, as are the three-hour terrain park and freestyle expression sessions.

Great:
For very good beginner and intermediate terrain, and family groups.

Not so great:
Real experts may tire of it after a couple of days.

HOW TO GET THERE

From Queenstown: It's 28 km or 45 minutes to drive there. Take Stanley Street from the town centre on to Frankton Road (State Highway 6A). At Frankton turn right onto SH 6. Carry on over the Kawarau River Bridge and past the Kelvin Heights turn-off; the Remarkables access road is a short drive further on.

From Wanaka: Take SH 6 past Cromwell and through the Kawarau River Gorge (beware of ice during winter) to Frankton. From here, the directions are as above.

Shuttle services operate from Queenstown on a regular basis. Contact the Queenstown Snow Centre, (03) 442 4640, for details.

SEASON:
LATE JUNE–
OCTOBER

Terrain Rating

Beginner	30%
Intermediate	40%
Advanced	30%

ALPINE HELI-SKI

ADDRESS

Alpine Heli-Ski, 34 Shotover Street, Queenstown
Telephone: (03) 441 2300 Email: ski@alpineheliski.com
Web: www.alpineheliski.com

THE SKI AREA

Alpine Heli-Ski operates out of Queenstown and transports powder hounds to 2000 sq Km of exclusively accessed terrain. Some of this territory includes the Hector and Eyre Mountains, Minaret Peaks, Mt Creighton and the Livingstone Mountains.

Skiers and boarders of intermediate level and above are grouped according to their ability and then flown to some of the most magnificent powder-covered slopes in the region. Alpine Heli-Ski maintains that if you can ski or board intermediate or blue runs, then you can heli-ski.

Guides at Alpine Heli-Ski are of the highest standard with plenty of experience in finding the best snow in the southern mountains. They hold industry qualifications and are trained in mountain safety and avalanche work, snowpack evaluation, ski guiding and rescue techniques. Their director holds an NZMGA certificate, the highest heli-ski guide qualification in New Zealand.

Powder skis are a lot wider than your standard carving skis, making it easier to turn in soft snow and giving much more stability in a wide range of conditions. It is recommended that snow boarders use a board 5–10 cm longer than they would normally use. Alpine Heli-Ski staff can supply you with a list of rental shops with the latest equipment.

At the beginning of each day Alpine Heli-Ski's director and snow safety officer will evaluate weather and snow conditions. Once the all-clear has been given, customers will receive a telephone call confirming operations, and a pick-up time from their accommodation. You will then be transported to the staging area, where you will be given a briefing on the use of an avalanche transceiver and all safety procedures for the day.

Briefing over, you board a high-performance Squirrel AS350BA/B2 or Hughes 500 helicopter and head out for the first runs of the day. These helicopters are preferred by Alpine Heli-Ski for their performance and manoeuvrability, required by their fully trained pilots in alpine flying.

SOUTHERN LAKES DISTRICT

SKIING AND BOARDING

The mountains of the Southern lakes region contain a vast area of terrain to choose from. A question always asked is, "Which run is the best?" This often depends on snow conditions and the weather of course, so I spoke to an owner and the Operations Manager of Alpine Heli-Ski; he had this to say:

'The Eyre Mountains south of Queenstown come to mind for a number of reasons. The area has spectacular scenery with steep U-shaped glacial valleys surrounded by high rock walls. The area initially appears intimidating as we fly guests into the first run, but for all its steepness there is run after run of wide open easy skiing down the glacial carved valleys. It is not uncommon for the Eyres to receive huge southerly dumps of snow when the areas further north receive only a few centimetres.

'The Long Burn would be my favourite run in the Eyres. The landing is high and a little precarious; as the helicopter approaches guests look at me and ask where he is going to land. I reassure them that it is OK and the chief pilot knows what he is doing. After the initial adrenalin rush subsides and everyone is in their skis and ready to go, we descend down an initial steep powder slope, keeping plenty of speed on to cross a wide flatter section. Then it is turn after turn of enjoyable skiing through gullies into a wide open valley and a long glide (hence the name) for over 2 Km down the valley to open flats, where our helicopter waits, ready to whisk us up to the next powder run. At the end of this run many guests typically say, "can we do that one again?"'

After that description I'll be there soon!

**SEASON:
JUNE–OCTOBER**

Terrain Rating

Beginner	0%
Intermediate	40%
Advanced	60%

Great:
Powder-hounds of intermediate level and above.

Not so great
Beginners.

HARRIS MOUNTAINS HELI-SKI

ADDRESS

Harris Mountains Heli-Ski, The Station, cnr Shotover
and Camp Streets, Queenstown
Telephone: (03) 442 6722 **Email:** hmh@heliski.co.nz **Web:** www.heliski.co.nz

THE SKI AREA

Harris Mountains Heli-Ski is one of New Zealand's oldest and most-respected heli-ski companies. HMH operates in the mountains around Queenstown and north to areas surrounding Wanaka and Aoraki/Mt Cook.

HMH's heli-skiing and heli-boarding terrain covers a vast area with more than 400 runs from in excess of 200 peaks in seven different mountain ranges. Each heli-run varies between 2000–3500 vertical feet, descending through sheltered basins, powder-filled bowls, steep chutes and wide mountain flanks. The company's area includes the Harris Mountains and Buchanans Range, and the Ben Ohau Range near Mt Cook.

Ideally suited to strong intermediate riders or better, HMH will assess your ability before placing you into a corresponding group. (After all, there's nothing more frustrating than finding you are out of your depth and holding back fellow skiers and boarders).

Each group consists of no more than five people escorted by a fully qualified and certified mountain guide. Prior to flying into the mountains, you will be issued with an avalanche transceiver and briefed on all safety matters. A buffet lunch is provided for you on the mountain.

HMH uses high-performance AS355 twin-engined and AS350 Squirrel helicopters. These machines have the highest CAA certification for alpine heli-ski operations and are flown by experienced pilots of the highest standard.

Powder snow in the Harris Mountains can be pretty deep. Although you can use your standard carving skis, it's a good idea to hire a pair of the latest wide-bodied powder skis; this will make for an easier day on your legs.

From Queenstown, HMH offer a range of heli-skiing and heli-boarding options, including:

Queenstown Experience This is a three-run deal especially suited to newcomers. Not too demanding and on terrain selected to suit your ability, this is a great introduction to heli-skiing.

Queenstown Classic A four-run day exploring some of the most awesome skiing and boarding terrain in the region. If you are still feeling fit after the four runs, you can upgrade to a couple of extra runs before flying back to the staging area.

Maximum Vertical A seven-run package for advanced skiers and boarders who want to go hard all day. Haven't had enough after seven runs? I am told that some of the Max Vert groups have been known to do 10–15 runs in a day!

Harris Mountain Heli-Ski has a number of other heli-ski options available from Queenstown, Wanaka and Mt Cook. Take a look at their website for prices and details or contact them by email.

Great:
For all skiers and boarders of at least an intermediate level.

Not so great:
Not very well suited for beginners.

SEASON: JUNE–OCTOBER ❄

Terrain Rating

Beginner	0%
Intermediate	35%
Advanced	65%

ADDRESS

Invincible Snowfields, Rees Valley Station, Glenorchy
Telephone: (03) 442 9933 Email: info@invincible.co.nz
Web: www.invincible.co.nz

INVINCIBLE SNOWFIELDS

THE SKI AREA

Elevation: 1800 metres
Vertical descent: **300 metres**
Skiable area: Heaps!

Let's get something straight right from the start: Invincible is not a ski area for wimps, for those who whinge about being too cold or for those who want groomed corduroy trails! Invincible Snowfields is for real skiers and boarders who do not mind roughing it a little. In return you'll have the time of your life on virtually your own private ski area.

About 50 Km from Queenstown near Glenorchy, Invincible Snowfields is a privately run concern on Rees Valley Station. Once you've arrived, it is apparent that there isn't any way into the ski area except by helicopter; hiking in is not an option, I'm told, because of the avalanche risk.

With some of the best back-country skiing and boarding in New Zealand, Invincible is a great alternative to the larger, more crowded ski areas. Here you will find no more than 10–20 people on the slopes serviced by a 700-m-long rope tow with a vertical descent of 300 m.

Invincible Snowfields are honest in their promotional material — they do not recommend the area as suitable for beginners or timid intermediates. The combination of a high-speed nutcracker tow and ungroomed snow would be too much for those inexperienced in skiing or boarding off-trail.

Invincible staff start the rope tow (powered by a tractor engine!) in 5th gear; once everyone has ridden it a few times they crank up the speed by dropping it into top gear.

For those of you who want to do a little hiking, the rewards are certain fresh lines in untracked powder on a good day.

For those staying overnight (highly recommended) there's a hut which sleeps 10 perched near the tow line. You will need to take essentials such as a sleeping bag and refreshments. The insulated hut has all the home comforts, including a pot-belly stove to warm up the place as you enjoy dinner and a few 'quiet ones' around the fire. Invincible Snowfields take pride in being environmentally sensitive too, so cooking is done on a gas burner while lighting is provided by a gas lamp or candles – very cosy! From the hut verandah you are treated to magnificent views of the surrounding mountains and valleys. Pack your camera.

Situated in the deep south of the main divide, Invincible gets a heap of cold powder, particularly from late June through to August, and superb spring snow later in the season. The main ski and boarding area has everything from wide open rolling slopes to steep gullies and chutes. Described as a natural terrain park, one snowboard magazine writer wrote that if you ever get the chance to session this place don't hesitate, not even for a second.

Invincible Snowfields operate on demand as conditions permit. Bookings are essential. It is a good idea to remember that if you are staying overnight, there is often the chance that you could get snowed in. Oh no! You might not be able to get to work for a day or two!

Great:
For hardy skiers and snowboarders wanting great snow, great terrain and no crowds. For those who want to get away from it all.

Not so great:
For beginners or for those inexperienced off-trail; if you don't enjoy 'roughing it'.

FACILITIES

- Helicopter into ski area
- 'Nutcracker' rope tow
- Accommodation on ski area

HOW TO GET THERE

From Queenstown: Take the road around Lake Wakatipu for around 50 km to Glenorchy. Follow the signs to the Rees Valley for another 15 km, until you arrive at the heli-pad which is well sign-posted.

If you'd rather not drive, Invincible may be able to arrange a helicopter flight from Queenstown for you.

SEASON: MID-JUNE–OCTOBER

Terrain Rating

Beginner	0%
Intermediate	25%
Advanced	75%

GLOSSARY

Boarder X course:	Competition involving a number of snowboarders racing a course all at once.
C-rail:	Curved terrain park feature on which tricks can be performed.
FIS:	International skiing federation (Fédération Internationale de Ski). World-governing body of all international skiing and snowboarding competitions.
Freeski:	Skiing or riding the whole mountain on all types of terrain.
Freestyle:	Terrain park boarding and skiing involving many tricks and manoeuvres.
Fun box:	Terrain park feature.
Gravity cross course:	Course where numbers of boarders race together.
Groomer:	Tracked vehicle that conditions and smoothes the snow surface.
Jibber:	Sliding on pipes, rails, boxes and other obstacles.
Kicker:	A bump or slope formed and used for aerial manoeuvres.
Lip:	Top edge of a pipe or half-pipe wall.
Magic carpet:	A beginner lift which operates like a conveyer or moving sidewalk.
Mogul:	A bump formed in the snow by skiers and boarders.
Nutcracker:	A steel object attached to a tow belt and shaped like a nutcracker.
Platter:	A lift that drags skiers and boarders up the hill.
Poma:	Similar lift to the above.
Quad chair:	Four-person chair lift.
Shredder:	Machine that shapes terrain park pipes.
Snow shoeing:	Cross-country walking through snow, aided by the use of snow shoes.
Snowcat:	Tracked vehicle used for snow transportation.
Super pipe:	Similar to a half pipe, but longer and with steeper walls.
T-bar:	An uphill two-person drag lift with a T-shaped bar.
Telemark:	Traditional skiing technique involving softer boots and freedom of heel lift during a turn.
Tow:	Rope tow. Usually a beginner lift where the skier or boarder grasps a rope, which then pulls them up a slope.
Twintipper:	A skier who utilises skis manufactured with 'twin tips', enabling many manoeuvres and techniques, usually on a terrain park.